ALONG THE RIVER KENT

CATHERINE ROTHWELL

The History Press

First published in 2005 by Sutton Publishing

Reprinted in 2012 by
The History Press
The Mill, Brimscombe Port,
Stroud, Gloucestershire, GL5 2QG
www.thehistorypress.co.uk

British Library Cataloguing in Publication Data

A catalogue record for this book is available from the British Library.

ISBN   978-0-7509-4131-0

Typeset in 10.5/13pt Galliard.
Typesetting and origination by
Sutton Publishing Limited.
Printed and bound in Great Britain by
Marston Book Services Limited, Didcot

Contents

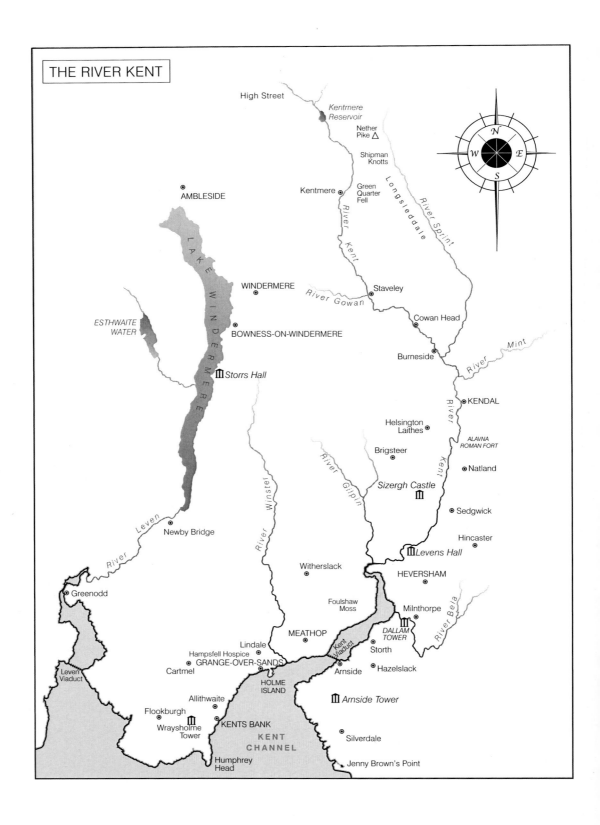

THE RIVER KENT

High Street

Kentmere Reservoir

Nether Pike △

Shipman Knotts

Kentmere

Green Quarter Fell

River Kent

Longsleddale

River Sprint

AMBLESIDE

L A K E   W I N D E R M E R E

WINDERMERE

River Gowan

Staveley

Cowan Head

BOWNESS-ON-WINDERMERE

ESTHWAITE WATER

Burneside

River Mint

Storrs Hall

River Kent

KENDAL

Helsington Laithes

ALAVNA ROMAN FORT

Brigsteer

Natland

River Winster

River Gilpin

Sizergh Castle

Sedgwick

Hincaster

River Leven

Newby Bridge

Levens Hall

Witherslack

HEVERSHAM

Greenodd

Foulshaw Moss

Milnthorpe

River Bela

MEATHOP

DALLAM TOWER

Lindale

Hampsfell Hospice

Kent Viaduct

Storth

GRANGE-OVER-SANDS

Cartmel

Arnside

Hazelslack

Leven Viaduct

HOLME ISLAND

Arnside Tower

Allithwaite

Flookburgh

Wraysholme Tower

KENTS BANK

KENT CHANNEL

Silverdale

Humphrey Head

Jenny Brown's Point

Foreword

With my late husband Eddie Rothwell, experienced teacher and fell walker, I made these forays into Kentmere following the courses of the Rivers Kent, Mint and Sprint but concentrating on the beautiful Kent. Glad I am that together we so relished those days spent over the seasons and the shared triumph of completing an enterprise.

Not long afterwards, Eddie fell victim to the cruel disease of cancer. These pages are written in tribute to him; he was a wonderful companion and photographer and is missed by so many, especially by his family.

Three generations of the Rothwell family leave the River Kent country after a day out in the summer of 1992, the aim – to initiate baby James in the art of fell walking. He woke up in time for the photograph! It was one of Eddie's last visits and James's first.

In ancient times known as the Cliff of Barath, St Bees Head is conspicuous and awesome, especially in storms. In 1718 a lighthouse was erected, and in 1823 a new light was installed with nine reflectors. In the eighteenth century a school of whales was stranded here. St Bees Head is one of only two Cumbrian limestone sea cliffs, rich in coral fossils which offered itself to small-scale industry, but the taking of fossils is now prohibited. Humphrey Head, the second cliff, is where the last wolf in England was reputedly cornered and killed. This beautiful engraving dates from 1839. (W.H. Bartlett)

Introduction

'In the making of books there is no end' states the Bible (Ecclesiastes 12:12) and perhaps this is to be expected when so much pleasure can be had from compiling books and, more hopefully, from reading them. This opinion is the result of personal experience. In following the River Kent from its source near High Street to 'the wide bay with the wondrous sands', we were more and more drawn to people we met, scenery unsurpassed and historical snippets from all those yesterdays to be mulled and wrangled over. It was a pity that, through lack of space, the latter had sometimes to be reduced to terse facts. There were anecdotes too numerous to recount, facts too full to chronicle and many happy encounters, although these could be stored in the memory to be savoured on dark, winter nights when Cumbrian country-roaming and following the river were out of the question.

There was Peter Hall's amusing story of Mr Paxton's primitive bobbin mill at Staveley and what happened when the factory inspector called (it was one man's job to 'turn off' the River Gowan and set it full sluice to the mill the following morning). There were also the tales of the 'travelling extraordinary' of Mr Unsworth, a Kendal policeman, who went from Kendal to Manchester and back in a day, 'a feat considered as bordering on the marvellous' in the year 1831; the Navvy Riots in 'the wilds of the Lake District'; the assizes attended by no fewer than 116 barristers at a test case concerning salmon fishing rights at Holme Hole, Milnthorpe sands; and Cropper's tramway to the Paper Mill at Cowen Head and how important it was when a penny per pound was taken off the duty on candles.

Even in the eighteenth century there were dreams of reclaiming Morecambe Bay, to make a coach road, immune from tides, across the delta-like estuary. Vagaries of weather, so vitally important to a farming community, ranged from a mighty flood of the River Kent when ground-floor rooms at Castle Mills were filled almost to the ceiling, through times of the river freezing, to a period of such severe drought that haymakers retreated from the burning sun and water supplies failed.

We experienced the thrill of seeing at close quarters a brass-faced Isaac Hadwen clock, inscribed '1724, Kendall'; had a welcome tea at the ancient High Close Farm, where we talked to Mrs Frank Salkeld on an April day when lambing time among the Kendal Roughs was imminent. Mrs Salkeld's father used to walk daily from Patterdale to Kentmere quarry, his place of employment – truly another case of 'travelling extraordinary'. Indeed, the people of Kentdale were travellers, probably sailing from Milnthorpe port. Newspapers reported voyages to Egypt, India and round the Horn. One Westmorland MP sailed for Bengal, 'not having vacated his seat or obtained leave of absence'. Jane Wilkinson died on board the ship *British Merchant* off the coast of Peru.

People impressed us with their love of their county, never taking such a wealth of beauty for granted; their awareness of heritage and their twinkling kindness. We met this everywhere, from the lady in the celebrated Kendal pie shop to the Robinsons at Guides Farm. Of such things is true contentment made and, in the making, as in that of books, here's hoping there will be no end.

Catherine Rothwell

SCATTERING ASHES ON HIGH STREET AT 2,719 FEET

Where curlews cry down the wind
Of soul-searching, echoing space,
There, to the bone are our beginnings,
Etched on the weatherworn stone.

Blood brothers, the Standard Bearers,
Marched moorlands where cotton grass bends,
And the Roman road's territory
Vanishes, into world's end.
Out of Kentmere, blowing wet, blowing dry
Like the sheep disguised as boulders
Day long we walked and called to one another,
Under the shaggy, changing Westmorland sky.

Curlew loud are the peaty-brown flashes.
'FLY DARLINGS – FLY'!
Their ashes flurry my face

But setting the pace
Together, road eager they vanish
They mingle in space.

1

'First Creeping Forth'

I first saw the region where the River Kent rises when I was seventeen years old and it remains a favourite because of its loneliness, its wide, wild horizons, especially towards High Street, and that thrilling link-thought 'the Romans were here'. We had approached from Patterdale, in the parish of which the Kent lies, on one of those changeable days when, out in the open, you blow wet and dry like the many sheep we encountered, which either stare in astonishment or lie snoozing disguised as boulders.

Warmed by bursts of sunshine and the freshness of the air, we felt we could walk for miles. Almost fifty years later enthusiasm had not waned but energy had. To write honestly of a river you must trace its source. That of the Nile was finally tracked down after years of effort on 14 November 1770. We were within sight of

Approaching the source of the River Kent.

the source of the Kent on 22 April 1987, not expecting to go down in history, but nevertheless feeling more triumphant than on that occasion, two years previously, when, approaching the source of the River Wyre, we were confronted by the unmistakable silhouette of a bull.

As I bought a pot of clover honey from the roadside lodge and explained my retreat, the proprietress admitted that she was in daily fear of going up field to feed her hens on account of that bull. It would appear that tracing river sources, like standing on one leg, is not easy, yet people must have found them all down the ages, because it is so satisfyingly obvious.

Cornelius Nicholson, in his *Annals of Kendal*, in succinct phrases tells us: 'The River Kent rises on High Street, a lofty mountain above Kentmere and running by Staveley, Burneside, Kendal, Sedgwick and Levens, falls into an estuary of the bay of Morecambe.' True, but it comes over as understatement and I prefer the poet Michael Drayton's words when he saw the source of Kent, or Can as it was named, in 1662: 'Can, first creeping forth, her feet hath scarcely found.' This man had a tender way of describing river sources, including the Lune, Wyre and Ribble, in their salmon-rich days. In travelling many counties he enumerated their features: buildings, birds, fishes, legends; but especially rivers, putting it all down in a poem of 1,500 lines – Polyolbion, which means 'having many blessings'. His aim was to awaken countrymen to the great beauties of England. A lovely way to spend an evening is reading Drayton, backed up by maps from William Camden's *Britannica*. Camden was the headmaster of Westminster School in the sixteenth century. He also liked to travel, making tours of antiquarian investigation in which he too visited the area of the River Kent.

Appropriately named, for it means 'from the high fells', in 1205 the word was spelled Kient. Subsequent spellings were Can, Kenet and Keent. Kentdale, through which the river flows, is one of the loveliest in the land and the river, a little over 20 miles from source to estuary, one of the most wildly beautiful. Celtic settlers deemed it 'the exalted river', also strikingly appropriate as its source is over 1,000ft above sea level.

Such a relatively short fall to the sea makes the Kent one of England's swiftest-flowing rivers, some think the swiftest, not a claim I dare make but one which I can believe, having seen the river in flood. Heavy rain over Kentmere can result, twelve to twenty-four hours later, in the dramatic sight of swirling branches, grasses tugged from banks, whole trees undermined and with their roots laid bare by the surge of turgid waters and withal a startling rise in river level. Autumn 1987, when salmon and sea trout were desperately battling upriver, as is their instinct, saw the Kent white with fury. Unmoved by the drama, a solitary heron watched from soaked, rocky outcrops, waiting for its moment to spear leaping fish from the tumbling river. It should be remembered that two hours before high water a spectacular bore rushes from Morecambe Bay, with the speed of a cantering horse, to meet the waters of the Rivers Kent, Gilpin and Bela flowing into the sea. High tides, strong winds and a swollen River Kent can flood roads to a depth of 2ft. Peaceful summer finds it flowing sweetly over a broad, limestone pavement base, with the wrack of winter still evident along its tide-marked banks. After much walking along them I grew to believe that, in its short course, the Kent produces more variety and excitement than most rivers, whatever the season.

Going for the source that April day, we set off from Kentmere village. It was in reaching the higher levels that the first frighteningly boggy stretch occurred and I was not surprised that fell ponies can lose shoes, tugged off by clinging, 'gungy' peat tussocks. Peat brown flashes lined with thick sedge, ravens in the sky and I, with my horror of mire and quicksands – it was good to reach firmer ground, to add stones to a cairn and suddenly come in sight of the awe-inspiring spread of High Street.

The source of the River Kent is where small becks tumble down the close contours of Wander Scar, Gavel Crag and Bleathwaite Crag. At Hall Cave, more becks join a waterfall. Froswick, Ill Bell, Kentmere Pike (2,397ft) and Shipman Knotts of the Kentmere Horseshoe all play their part in this catchment area. As exhorted by that guru of the fells, Mr A. Wainwright, in one of his books, we girded up our ancient loins and, map in hand, found traces of the Roman ridge road that makes its way towards Racecourse Hill in line with the Kendal camp at

The view from Ill Bell. On the right is the Roman road.

Watercrook and links with Low Borrow Bridge. It follows a steep gradient to the line of crags then runs at 2,200ft above sea level. Amid such desolate majesty it took little imagination to picture the legions swinging sturdily behind the standard bearers, all primed with their morning porridge.

I forgot to mention that on the way up, about 2 miles from Badger Rock, we found the perfect place for lunch: a rock table and chair fashioned by nature. Backed by crags with views all around, sheltered in the lee of boulder erratics, we could hear the clear carrying sounds of dogs barking in the valley. Munching silverside of beef sandwiches, tomato, watercress and fruit with hot coffee to follow and a clear beck beside us hurrying off to join the Kent, what more could the heart desire?

In the tenth century the Norsemen came to stare, hawk-eyed at the Silurian rocky outcrops, tumbled scree, marshland, bog, moor grass, sphagnum mosses and lichens. They probably sailed into Morecambe Bay and up the Kent estuary. Hundreds of place names with Norse derivations survive. Hard Knott means hard hill, streams are becks and farms garths. The words thwaite, tun, rigg and toft give clues to banished trades and ownerships. There are the remains of other civilisations in Kentmere but it is the pele towers that predominate, examples being Burneside Hall, Skelsmergh Hall, Godmond Hall and Selside Hall, which were built to protect people and animals from bellicose Scottish raiders. Over those crags came the marauders and later, with their cattle from Scotland, along a drove road, Scot Take, would come more peaceful individuals: the drovers and the pedlars known as 'Scotchmen', although these last-termed were not always from that country. All would see the peregrines, buzzards, kestrels, kites, dippers, ravens and crows wheeling in the skies, the foxes, red squirrels, red deer and hares ranging the fells. Sadly, in our time, the charming green lizards have all but vanished.

In the nineteenth century another posse burst into Kentmere when it was decided to dam the waters of the river, thus creating Kentmere Head Reservoir and ensuring a steady supply of power to turn mill wheels along the Kent. Mercifully the Kent remains a beautiful river despite the hand of man, and to follow it from source to sea, throughout all seasons, was a rewarding experience. Kentmere itself, although considered less impressive than the beetling crags of the Lake District, is, I think, more to be desired, especially at the height of summer, than the booted, rucksacked enclaves of Ambleside and Keswick. They say great things happen when men and mountains meet. Climbing to the source in sight of High Street, we saw only one other young walker, an intrepid young man striding the fell in a northerly direction.

KENTMERE VILLAGE

Kentmere village is a handy spot to park the car prior to walking, but make sure you are there early, for space by the Kentmere Institute, built in 1926, is limited. The church of St Cuthbert, nearby, is at least 400 years old; parts of the building may be Norman or even Saxon. It was re-roofed in the sixteenth century and the church bell cast in the seventeenth. Before the church's restoration in 1866 this bell probably hung, as was usual, in a bell cote. Did the remains of the body of St Cuthbert rest

Kentmere, 1900. The white building in the foreground was a temperance hotel.

here when the Lindisfarne monks were moving around the north of England in their attempt to steer clear of the Danish invaders? Legend holds that wherever the body rested before its final incarceration at Durham the monks raised a cross or church. Kentmere was settled at that time; Neolithic, Celtic and Norse evidence has been found. On the range between Longsleddale and Kentmere, at High Borrans, are the stone heaps of an early British settlement.

Our September visit coincided with a Festival of Flowers at St Cuthbert's depicting the rich flora and fauna of Kentmere: a magnificent setting for the clear-glass East window, which looks across the valley to the farms of Green Quarter and the ever-changing fells. On that day they were a glorious russet shade, lit up by sudden sunshine.

A long flash of water, all that remains of Kentmere, alongside a stretch of the river close to the village, is best viewed from on high en route to the source. Over 140 years ago it was drained to provide more land for cultivation and pasture, for practically the whole valley was drowned. The lake is gradually re-establishing itself, but when first dried out, a valuable diatomaceous earth was discovered, forming the basis for a unique industry – diatomite, an insulating material that can withstand high temperatures. This was processed on the site now operated by British Industrial Sands.

Kentmere was described in 1577 as 'a poole a myle compass' and, in 1692 by Thomas Machell, another traveller around Westmorland, as being half a mile long and a haven for wild swans and duck. Drainage brought to light two dugout canoes and a Viking spearhead: evidence of early settlement.

Kentmere Hall, built in the fourteenth century, is one of many pele towers. Much damaged and now a farm, it was once the home of the Gilpin family. The story is told of Hugh Hird, 'cork lad of Kentmere', who, during its reconstruction, put into place, unaided, a 30ft oak beam which ten men were struggling to position. Hugh was noted for such feats of strength, but they took their toll and he died young, unlike the Revd Bernard Gilpin who had wily brains rather than brawn. Although brought up a Catholic, he embraced the Protestant faith under Henry VIII and was known as the Apostle of the North. He entertained in grand style at Kentmere Hall, giving an ox to poor parishioners at Christmas. Even when called to account, he managed to break a leg, rendering himself unfit to travel. His persecutor, Roman Catholic Queen Mary, died in the interim and Queen Elizabeth I, who succeeded her, accepted his views. Able to return to his succulent barons of beef, he did not die until 1583, aged about 70. His generosity enabled some Westmorland boys to become well educated and influential.

FARMS

Browfoot Farm is typical of Kentmere farms, nestling snugly in sheltered hollows. The Westmorland Gazette reported on 29 October 1849, the year that Queen Adelaide died, that on a farm in Kentmere the snow lay as far down as the house door until 11 June and again made its appearance on the same spot on 3 October, 'producing a summer of sixteen weeks and ten days for the occupants'. Rain rather than snow was what we encountered in 1987, but weather patterns are changing.

Goose Howe Farm.

Westmorland shepherd, 1890.
(G.P. Abraham)

A breed of long-horned black cattle was common in the seventeenth century and, although there are still beef and dairy cattle, sheep are more important; Rough Fell and Kendal Rough, sturdy, broad-backed and with black faces, are the local pure breed. They graze on 'heafs', grassed areas between 50 and 1,000ft up, which they learn to recognise and from which they do not stray. The 1936 caterpillar plague in Kentmere drove the sheep from high pastures. Long ago, when wolves lurked, it is said that tender sprigs of holly and ash were fed to the flocks, producing mutton of remarkably fine flavour. Consequently, the holly was tended and revered. Of all the old postcards of shepherds, with sheep draped like scarves around their necks, I thought the best was the one of the twinkling-eyed Kentmere shepherd that is used as the Abbot Hall Art Gallery and Museum motif.

Until twenty years ago sheep shearing was done by hand, with the clippers moving from farm to farm. On the large fields alongside the lake, sheepdog trials are held every September. The craftsmen of Kentmere include dry-stone wall builders and, according to an expert, Mr Frankland of Ravenstonedale, the majority of farmers still have considerable skills at this and pass it down from father to son. Dry-stone walls consist of 'face' stones and 'fillings'. The biggest, roughest stones are placed on the bottom, usually 28in wide and tapering to 18in at the top, which must be level so that the sheep will not jump over. Going right through the walls are 'through' stones, sometimes mistakenly thought to be stiles, but which protrude simply because it is difficult to cut stone exactly. A two-ended hammer, with sharp and square edges, is the main tool used. The Celts had a quite different system, placing long stones (orthostats) on end into the ground and filling the gaps between with rubble.

Near Badger Rock, a collection of huge, heather-grown stones, were two lichen-covered tall stones serving as gateposts, each with two round holes cut into their tops. These were perhaps once used for tethering horses or fell ponies. In repairing the dry-stone walls, many of which have stood for over a century, old clay pipes have been found hidden inside, maybe left by Irish navvies turning their hands to dry-stone walling when canal building had passed in the early nineteenth century.

A report of a local hiring fair, held on 10 June 1848, states: 'More young persons offered themselves for hire than was ever before witnessed and the streets at times were almost impassable'. Wages then ranged from £12 15s a year for male farm workers and £6 10s for women servants. At these fairs, known in some places as Mop Fairs, held on Michaelmas Day in the market square or main street, men wishing

Dancing around the maypole at the Westmorland Fair, c. 1930.

A Kentmere kitchen.

to be hired wore a sign in their hat bands: shepherds wore a lock of wool, carters a wisp of horse hair, clerks an inkhorn. Hiring was over at midday and was signalled by the ringing of the church bell. The symbol of deals struck was by the hirer handing over a shilling. The arrangement was legally binding for twelve months, according to custom, and could be broken only by 'running away' within ten days, so that in some areas another hiring fair, 'the runaway mop', was held.

Mr R.E. Smith, whose father, mother and grandfather were hired for farmwork in Kentmere – and he himself was hired early last century when £2 was paid for six months' work – told me that the local expression was 'taking urdles'. He remembers rising at 5.30 a.m., washing under the pump, wiping down with a piece of sacking and being so hungry that he ate nettles, docks and hawthorn leaves (otherwise known as 'bread and cheese'), wild strawberries and 'tewit's' eggs, while working the fields, until the farmhouse meal at 6 p.m. Stores of clap bread and oak cakes were kept in bread cupboards in the slate-floored Kentmere farm kitchens. Beside the range was often a spice cupboard of black oak carved with a date and initials from the seventeenth or eighteenth centuries. Mr Smith, a one time cowman on farms overlooking the Kent estuary, recalled his favourite – 'fiddle pastry' made from ends of dough stuffed with currants. Longevity was notable. Henry Kelley died in 1720, aged 116; Christian Modesty on 25 November 1802, aged 114, and one newspaper cutting mentions 'four widows' whose ages totalled over 400 years.

Plough matches put the lads on their mettle; one on 15 March 1835 involved seventeen ploughs. Of twelve prizes awarded one went to the son of Richard Stainton

'Sexton Joe', 1890.

of Fellside, Sizergh. Harvest time found many Irish crossing to Cumberland and Westmorland. Old photographs show that the toothed sickle was favoured for efficient harvesting, even though more bending was involved than with the scythe. In the photograph opposite 'Old Joe' the sexton, who seems a good stand-in for 'death the reaper', appropriately wields the scythe.

There were cheese fairs, horse, cattle and flower shows. A Christmas cattle fair could dispose of 300 cows and 500 sheep, 'flesh days' indeed; beef sold at 4½d to 6d per lb, mutton from 5*d* to 6*d* per lb.

Of the many ancient farming customs few or none remain, although a 'boon day' was organised in April 1937 at Johnscales in the Lyth Valley. It was customary to help an incoming tenant and Mr G.E. Machell had the services of twenty men from the district when he moved into his farm.

PACKHORSE WAYS

Two important routes lie close to St Cuthbert's church: westward over Garburn to Troutbeck and beyond; eastward to Green Quarter Fell into Longsleddale, seen in snow in 1971, the lonely, beautiful valley contiguous to Kentmere. Southward the way ran to the coast while to the north it headed for Shap and Penrith over Nan Bield Pass. The Lindisfarne monks may have trodden one or other of these ancient routes that were later used by the long packhorse trains and itinerant pedlars.

During the summer of 1987 Janet Niepokojczycko, with her black packhorse, William Wordsworth, retraced 450 miles of eighteenth-century packhorse roads in

Longsleddale in snow, 1971.

Cumbria, raising money for the charity Search. It was hoped that £2,000 could be raised for the group's Special Heritage Appeal on archaeology in Kentmere, Search having discovered evidence of a 1,200-year-old Viking settlement.

Fell ponies are descended from Celtic ponies which, with exposure to storms, developed tough constitutions. By the Middle Ages they were being used as packhorses to carry wool, coal, cloth and liquor. Some worked underground in lead mining or pulled carts and ploughs. Popular today for pony trekking, the true-bred Lakeland animal is friendly and intelligent and has straight, strong legs, a large girth, long mane and tail. The poet Robert Southey said that pedlars' packs often contained French toys made of bone and contraband such as wines and spirits. A long, lonely seaboard with many creeks and harbours made smuggling easier.

Nineteenth- and early twentieth-century carting was handled by the Clark family of Kendal, using covered horse wagons to deliver in Milnthorpe and Kentmere. Another useful service was that of the travelling tailor, James Thompson, in the 1870s, who called on farms and houses with a horse and trap and willing to make a suit for 3s 6d if the farmer supplied his own material.

LONGSLEDDALE

Sleddal was probably the Norseman who settled in the valley next to Kentmere, a valley not to be missed on account of its beauty and its river's close link with the Kent. Most of it used to be owned by Shap Abbey. Of twenty-four chapelries in Kendal parish one was Longsleddale. The church, built in 1863, possesses an Elizabethan chalice and paten from 1571; and it would seem that a medieval chapel served a thirteenth-century community busy in the wool trade. In this valley of the River Sprint, which rises high in the fells near Haweswater, and is said to be the swiftest-flowing river in England – 'the running, bounding river' relegates Kent to second in the lists. The church and school are on the road running parallel to it. The old school closed in 1942, the children being transferred to Selside school by taxis.

The story of The School on the Fells is told by Olwen Harris, its last headmistress, with the atmosphere being reminiscent of Laura Ingalls Wilder's book, *The Little House on the Prairie*. Mrs Humphrey Ward loved Longsleddale, considering it one of Westmorland's best valleys, and featured it as Long Whindale in her book Robert Elsmere. She was visiting in 1885 when the lanes were white with blackthorn blossom. The packhorse track passes Kilnhouse Farm, once a sixteenth-century inn, and there is a packhorse bridge across the Sprint at Sadgill.

Seventeenth-century farms on each side of the river include Ubarrow Hall with its remains of a pele tower. The 'deep long valley' (slead is Old English for valley) reminded me of the Langstrath in Borrowdale, but is more beautifully wooded. An interesting historical entry about Longsleddale concerns John Mattinson, a schoolmaster said to have been the 'terror and delight' of his pupils. He was 'unfortunately shott', which leaves one wondering. Other records reveal that John and Isaac Hudson of Longsleddale were drowned bathing on the Sands on 24 June 1792, both aged 16, a fate which also overtook two farm workers returning from a hiring fair.

2

Water Power

From its source, through Kentmere, the reaches of the river look peaceful, picturesque and wholly taken over by nature, but for centuries these waters had to work. The demands of the Industrial Revolution and those of hundreds of years before caused man to harness the River Kent for his own ends. Like Furness, with its mining of haematite ore and charcoal burning, Kentmere was a busy area. The peaceful delights of nearby Borrowdale and the Bannisdale valleys and the serenity of the hills round Kentmere Horseshoe belie such industrialism, but it is obvious that over a century ago the authorities were concerned about the decline of fish stocks. In May 1887, 5,000 new trout were obtained through the London-based Fish Culture Association, to be released into the River Kent and its tributaries. 'It would be interesting to know', records the *Westmorland Gazette*, 'what the new fish think of their habitat which has been of a deep coffee colour due to discolouration through dyes.' Since men lived in caves, 'Salar, the leaper', as the Romans called the salmon, has surged up rivers to spawn, but pollution, poaching and trawling out at sea have drastically cut what was once a bountiful supply. Alarming statistics from the River Kent alone show: 1966, 2,300 fish taken on rod and line; 1976, a drought year, fewer than 400; 1984, 687. Canoeing and angling clubs use reaches of the river, where it glides at its own sweet will. Notices nailed onto trees show how these rights are jealously guarded.

Man's best friend, however, is surely the sheep, for it has clothed, fed and, for centuries, been an outstanding source of wealth for him – witness the land's great 'wool churches', Kendal's being one. The wool industry supported whole communities living on the banks of the Kent and its tributaries. At Sadgill in Longsleddale there was a fulling mill in 1297, while Garnett Bridge at the dead end of this vale had two mills, one of which operated until 1916.

In our walks we found the tumbledown remains of small stone buildings. Waterwheels and millstones, now relics, have been fitted into walls, paths, barns or used nostalgically in garden settings. Once upon a time they served to generate power for the concentrated Kentmere industrial area, at its peak in the mid-nineteenth century: industries such as corn, bobbin, paper, snuff, textile and leather mills, most of them now no more. This chapter explores those that remain and the happy changes and adaptations to the needs of a different century.

Draining the mere in 1841 led to a reduction of water force for the mills so it was decided to dam the waters of the Kent to create Kentmere Head reservoir under 'An

Old millstones used in a water garden, Staveley, Kentmere.

Act for Maintaining Reservoirs in the Parish of Kendal'. The original plan involved the Mint and the Sprint also, but the 1848 reservoir cost almost £14,000 so only one was completed. On Potter Fell, Gurnal Dubbs, Ghyll Pool and the artificial Potter Tarn were adapted for industrial purposes, supplying James Cropper and Company who now have exclusive rights on the fell.

Some small, disused mills have been converted into beautiful riverside homes. Beck Mills, once water-powered, was offered for sale in 1987, its conversion using the mill head and tail races as unique features in the grounds which comprise half of the river bed on their frontage for salmon and trout fishing. The owner of this desirable residence, made outstandingly beautiful by natural rocky banks and deep river pools, the wheel house now a hobby room, could truly quote Jonathan Swift:

> . . . a handsome house to lodge a friend,
> a river at my garden's end.

On a very wet July afternoon my husband and I visited another riverside sawmill, which has become Rural Craft Studio, producing Kentmere Pottery. Gordon and Barbara Fox specialise in exquisite, hand-painted English enamels and ceramic decoration using glowing lustres and precious metals. Sure enough another preserved millstone was propped up outside Sawmill Cottages.

The justly famous Westmorland green slate needs skilled craftsmen to work it and it could be seen in the wishing well featured at the Kentmere Church Flower Festival. Disused quarries on the route to Kentmere Head reservoir (useful shelter for eating your sandwiches out of the wind) are a reminder of the nineteenth and twentieth centuries' quarrying to supply important buildings in London and elsewhere.

Bismin, the industrial division of British Sand, is a present-day Kentmere industry. Plans to obtain more of the commercially valuable diatomite from Skeggle Water on Green Quarter Fell were strongly objected to for fear of environmental damage and the idea was dropped.

Not far from Barley Bridge, where there was an early corn mill, Kentmere Ltd flourishes on the site of a twelfth-century fulling mill. As we walked past I eyed the sign with affection for I remembered that my father, fifty years ago, bought all the photographic supplies for his business from this paper firm, which still has a photographic division.

Because our first attempt to reach the Kent's source was thwarted, the road to Kentmere village being closed for some weeks in the spring of 1987, we parked at Scrogg's Bridge to explore in another direction. We were never far from the river, noting the weir at Barley Bridge and the fascinating, glassy flow of water just before it plunged to the churned river below. No coffee-coloured discolouration here! It was clear and limpid. Climbing a narrow lane, we passed a red-haired girl with three red setter dogs (diarist Thomas Tyldesley might have said: 'a sight I never saw before!') whose smile seemed to express her love of life and the whole beauty of the day. Indeed, this walk was so marvellous in spring we came back in autumn to see berry-laden rowans, bracken-brown slopes, hazel nuts, blackberries, harebells, ragged robin, Queen Anne's lace, seeded foxgloves and the last of the wild roses. Rooks cawed insistently and a band of coloured chaffinches plundered and gorged thistledown from gaunt plants. Above the sound of the Kent rushing over boulders

The River Kent towards Kendal, 1904.

came the plaintive cries of sheep mingling with a wind in the trees that sounded like the sea. Before the morning was out on our autumn ramble, we had to retreat as a black bull appeared on the skyline, somewhat overshadowing the beautiful play of light and shade passing over the low fells.

STAVELEY

As early as 1136 a fulling mill operated at Barley Bridge and by the thirteenth century there were no fewer than six situated at Staveley. Because of its drop in height the River Kent was found to be ideal and, with its tributaries, had a total of sixty mills. Some were very old, others built in the eighteenth century, but the only remaining mill using water power is the snuff mill at Helsington, although this was used until 1971 in the wool trade at Staveley. Today woodworking and furniture being made by hand can be watched at Peter Hall Woodcraft on Danes Road, Staveley, where meticulous craftsmanship reveals the natural figure in oak and mahogany. At Staveley, which means 'a wood where staves are cut', the river Gowan flows into the Kent and once powered seven mills on its banks. In 1281 William de Thweng granted the town the right to hold a market on Fridays and a three-day fair from 17 to 19 October; Gala Sunday was on 28 June in 1987.

Wood carver, Peter Hall & Son, Staveley.

Of the church of St Margaret, originally built in 1388, all that remains is the tower with damaged windows, which it is hoped will soon be restored. Another church, St James's, built in 1864, further up the road to Kentmere and opposite present-day mills, contains a stained-glass window designed by the pre-Raphaelite, Burne-Jones, the glass coming from William Morris's Kelmscott Studio.

In the old church, of which only the tower remains, a meeting of yeoman farmers was held on 2 January 1620. They were protesting against the abolition by James I of border tenants' rights. John Smith, the High Constable, and 100 Staveley men brought the case but they had a fight of five years before the Star Chamber Court settled in their favour. The many laws covering tenant rights were added to by Enclosure Acts: over 1,500 private Enclosure Acts were passed by Parliament between 1760 and 1797. There even existed 'basket tenure', the tenant of such a holding being required to make baskets for the Crown.

All towns are made more interesting by having a railway station and that at Staveley, being set so high, affords very good views of town and countryside, even looking down on the roof of the Railway Hotel alongside. In 1948 the signal box was burned down. A quarter of a mile down the line from the railway crossing over the A591 a station was built to serve the village of Kentmere, which is three miles up the valley. Until 1967 the crossing had hand-operated gates but, at least a dozen times, trains crashed through them when signals had become stuck in the wrong position. Early LMS red liveried locomotives were a common sight in the 1920s on the branch line between Staveley and Burneside.

On the main road out of Staveley, not far from the Kent, is Stock Bridge Farm with its date stone declaring 1638. One of the duties of the High Constable of Staveley was to inspect bridges over the river. Since 1530 a county rate was allowed for the repair of bridges outside towns that were not the responsibility of an authority or person. Since time immemorial no one has ever been anxious to claim ownership because that would have meant the steady expense of repair. Money paid for the upkeep of local bridges was known as Brighote. What an interesting study the bridges spanning the Kent would make! A hundred years ago tradesmen crossing to Bridge End cottages, in the days when Staveley was a market town, would include shearers, tanners, cordwainers, skinners, tailors, barbers and paviors (men paid by the town to see to the upkeep of paving stones). Churchwardens acted as overseers of the poor, doling out parish relief and entering it into account books. Some help was also given to 'maimed soldiers'. In 1843 the salary of the beadle was raised to £39. Other officers included ale tasters, flesh lookers and leather sealers, but one unpopular officer, after taking a debtor to prison, was seized, 'dragged to the pump and pumped upon'.

BURNESIDE

Staveley Park runs alongside the Kent and on a muggy July day, as we approached Burneside, millions of midges were swarming above the public footpath. A pleasant footpath at Carlingdale, through flowery meadows, led to Kendal, but we were bent on exploring the river at its commercial heart, which in Burneside means only one thing – James Cropper plc – reflecting on a great success story. Since 1845 the little township has been linked with this family. The original James Cropper, a Quaker from Liverpool, married into the Wakefield family and as a young man managed a business that was to become one of the most important makers of strong paper and board in the world. Besides the Burneside Mill, James also worked a paper mill at Cowan Head on the River Kent, which in the 1820s had been owned by Cornelius Nicholson, author and part publisher of Annals of Kendal. Other businessmen, including John Bryce (the Bryce Institute is in the village), aided James in efforts to increase the supply of water to the mills by damming. Together they got the aforementioned Act through parliament. When James died in 1900 he had seen an enormous expansion of his business but was spared the heartache of Burneside Mill's destruction by fire in 1903. Despite this setback the firm's aim, 'making paper with a purpose', continued to flourish. More discarded millstones were seen on the large complex, presumably from original water mills on the Kent. We saw outbuildings dated 1856, an 1872 drinking fountain for horses, a memorial to 'fellow workmen in two world wars', plus terraces of pleasant houses for workpeople, all of which expressed a successful, long-established family concern. Tours of this paper mill were arranged: its accessibility is not surprising as it is the forebear of them all.

In a field opposite Carling House, near Junction Cottages, we photographed the confluence of the Rivers Kent and Sprint. Does Junction Cottages, which could

Junction Cottages, Burneside.

have been used for tollhouse purposes, refer to road or river junction? Nicholson's Annals of Kendal refers to Burneside Hall as 'standing on a tongue of land formed by the junction of the Kent and Sprint'. Another thirteenth-century pele tower, now a farmhouse, Burneside Hall, occupied what was the ancient manor of Strickland Roger. The family home of the de Burnesheads, it was also lived in by the Bellinghams and the Cliffords, powerful local names, as indeed is that of James Winstanley Cropper who later bought it. Another family in its long history was the Braithwaites, one member of which, 'Drunken Barnaby', brought dubious fame. Richard Braithwaite's journal, in somewhat doggerel verse, describes his bibulous journeys in the north-west, although the wine may not, as he implies, have flowed as freely as the Kent waters.

The gateway to Burneside Hall.

James Cropper, 'the last MP for the ancient borough of Kendal'.

The 1856 vicarage next to the church and close neighbour of the great mill complex has typical round, Westmorland chimneys. The church itself, noted for its woodwork, possesses a fine stained-glass window, 'Risen Lord', installed in 1936. Charles I's reign has mention of Burneside's original 'chapelle' erected in 1602. In 1756, £200 from Queen Anne's Bounty was granted to buy more land, but the church was not actually built until 1826. However, James Cropper, desiring a church 'worthy of Burneside', pulled down his barns and built a great edifice. The 1826 building was demolished and, in 1881, St Oswald's arose on the site of the 1602 chapel, a fragment of whose wall can still be found. Gravestones of the Cropper family go back to the 1820s, assembled like the Wordsworth family's in Grasmere churchyard, but simpler in style.

Margaret Cropper, friend and biographer of Evelyn Underhill, died in 1980 at Laurel Cottage, Burneside. She was indeed a gifted poet, reminiscent of Wordsworth in her long, evocative poems of the Westmorland countryside and her sensitivity towards its people whose character she appreciated.

Across the way from James Cropper plc, what was once a tiny school by the river bears a stone tablet, readable only through binoculars: 'This school was rebuilt by the benefaction of the Revd Allan Fisher of Hundow in Strickland Roger who bequeathed £600 for its endowment and departed this life 16 May, aged 84'. Amid so much history – and the river has seen it all – lorries, bearing the Cropper logo

The River Kent, downstream from New Bridge, near Sedgwick.

Bannisdale in snow, c. 1970. The lonely valley which sorts the women from the girls.

of doves, thunder down the supply road to Technical Fibres Products Section. We turned for home as rain set in for the day, to return in autumn for a 7-mile walk along the Kent, passing mills at Cowan Head and Bowston. With the long line of the Howgill Fells above Kendal on our left etched slate grey against the sky, we savoured a lazy evening watching an old John Wayne western. It seemed a fitting end to the day.

THE RIVER MINT

Bannisdale joined our short list of secret valleys. Secluded by trees from the many A6 travellers it has remained relatively unknown. According to Wainwright it is 'a favourite grazing ground for fell ponies'. Overlooked by burly White Howe, Bannisdale Beck joins the River Mint flowing past signs of ancient settlements (Robin Green) among which are clear remnants of hut circles. One senses an atmosphere of a valley that time forgot, changeless in appearance throughout eons of time.

One interesting story was encountered because a few local people have relics of the happening to prove it, to this day (or so we were told). In 1745, here, an ammunition wagon of a once-marching army was overturned. Bonnie Prince Charlie's dispirited groups of stragglers, winding north after great disappointment, must have thought it the last straw. Cannonballs spewed off the wagon and cascaded down the rough track. Some of the ammunition was retrieved later when the weary Highlanders had reloaded the wagon and became treasured, if grim, mementoes. I like that story passed down the generations but, until I see one of those cannonballs, it remains in the cupboard with those about the number of beds slept in by Queen Elizabeth I.

THE RIVER SPRINT

The Sprint passes Kentmere Pike. It is Longsleddale country and reminded us of the Langstrath Valley in Borrowdale. Am I walking to the world's end? Is there no end? I wondered. Eight miles in length, the walk included a mingling fear, excitement and a sense of the staggering beauty of majestic fell country, especially when snowbound.

Where the River Kent and River Sprint meet.

When one is almost at the end of one's tether, towering ramparts threaten, almost shouting: 'Don't get ideas, petty earthling. I've been here longer than you and I shall be here when you are gone – I am the boss.' Trapped within such thoughts lies the lure of high hills. The narrowness of this valley with its steeply rising fell sides gives the River Sprint its claim to fame as the swiftest flowing river, one having few tributaries apart from Stockdale Beck. Thank goodness this country of golden eagles was not despoiled by a reservoir. Sprint's glory also lies in its waterfalls and cascades. Mills from many moons ago used the fast-flowing waters of the River Sprint. Abandoned weirs and mill races remain which, to my mind at least, add to the romance and mistiness of the years.

3

'Where Kendal Town doth Stand'

O f many settlers, the Saxons used the name Kirkby-Candale, 'the church
town on the banks of the chief river', to mark Kendal. The Normans
divided the barony of Westmorland: Grasmere, Ambleside and Windermere
being in the barony of Kendal, while Appleby represented the other half. Archives
therefore include widespread references. The grassy mounds on Castle How, but a
short walk from the town centre, were considered in Nicholson's day to be of Saxon
or Roman origin, but thoughts were voiced with conviction in 1907 that there had
been a motte and bailey castle built by the Normans. What is certain is that this

The River Kent at Kendal before the changes to the river bank.

This is how old Kendal looked when Egg Tommy hawked baskets of fresh eggs. R. Rawes was the licensee at the Rose and Crown Inn. Many interesting signs include W. Cragg, Clog and Patten Maker (notice the large model of a boot on the wall); Walmsley, Cabinet Makers and Upholsterers; Mr Boddington, Hosier. In the foreground is a man selling water from a barrel. The entrance leads to a yard or weind, many of which go back to the medieval period and were built behind the main streets throughout their length. The archway could be closed at night by a massive oak door, possibly at one time a defence against Scottish invaders. Many of the workers from the woollen industry lived in these yards, Kendal being a very important woollen town. Doctor Manning's Yard in Highgate is one of the few remaining examples.

position and that of Castle Hill on the other side of the River Kent, where rose a securely built Norman castle in stone, are strategically well placed.

In our two-castle walk, ably set out in Kendal Deanery Walks, we first sought the motte and bailey castle on the Howe, which was probably constructed between 1068 and 1100. I fully expected another bull, avenging descendant from those once baited and slaughtered on Beasts' Bank which we traversed, but commanding views of the town were enjoyed unhindered over to the Lake District Fells and the Pennines.

By the time the river reaches Kendal, joined by Anchorite Wells Beck, Blind Beck and the River Mint, it has assumed a broad, businesslike flow. Black-headed gulls were flying up from the sea on a raw, cold day in March 1988 as we overlooked the line of fells, icing-white from freshly fallen snow, from Nether Bridge (Caput Pontis). Records show again and again that, besides being an efficient servant, the river could disastrously overflow its banks. Almost a year before Kendal's first mayor, Thomas Sleddale, took office, the Kent rose into the church vestry and, on the following stormy day, forty-eight men and women, including the ferryman, Thomas Miller, plus nine horses, were drowned in Windermere. In John Towers' mayoralty, 'the wooden bridge having been carried away by flood', another was built on stone pillars. After many inundations it became imperative to raise the road level at Stramongate by an embankment. These, and other events in a long and stimulating history, are listed in a chronological table of the Chief Magistrate of the 'burgh of Kirkly-in-Kendal' from its first important incorporation in 1575. In our time, the year 1987 witnessed archaeological investigation funded by English Heritage: thirteenth- and fourteenth-century pottery was found and the remains of sequences of timber buildings with beautifully cobbled yards. Kendal's huge fund of history, much of which stems from the river, fills books. This chapter can merely comment on features in plan, purpose and relationships to the river by touching on church, castle, market, streets and trades.

KENDAL PARISH CHURCH

Even to begin to know Kendal many visits are necessary and we had the good fortune on our second to meet Mr J. Clements, Church Husband of the parish church dedicated to the Holy Undivided Trinity. He drew our attention to the 'not

The River Kent near the parish church, Kendal.

to be missed': fifteen beautiful angels aloft, carved when the church was re-roofed in 1868; an eighth-century fragment of an Anglican cross near the fourteenth-century aisle built for the Flemish weavers who settled; the helmet ascribed to fiery Robin the Devil; and the clerestory with the oldest stained glass.

Mr Clements, who was baptised, in 1907, in the fifteenth-century black marble font, sang in the choir ten years later and has since had an unbroken association with the church. Nineteenth-century restoration uncovered a parchment dated 1226, but the first church was built in Kirkland on Kent's west bank as early as the ninth century. The Domesday Book reference in 1086 reads Cherchebi. Today's building, with thirty-two pillars, square embattled tower and five aisles, is recognisable as a great 'wool' church like that of Chipping Norton. It is the second widest parish church in the country, lovingly restored over years.

When Kendal was burned and pillaged by the Scots in 1210, at the time of the 6th Baron, not only was the church ransacked but women and children seeking sanctuary were, according to Holinshed's Chronicles, put to the sword. Of the brasses in Kendal church – and the favourite of brassrubbers is Alan Bellingham, knight in armour – one reveals that Frances Strickland, born 1690, married 1708, died 1725, experienced all these events on the same calendar date, 24 June. Walking around this light, clear-windowed church, you are aware of names that made Kendal famous: Bellingham; Parr; Strickland. Close to the chapel of the latter lies Thomas West, author of *Antiquities of Furness* and friend of the Stricklands, who died at Sizergh Castle in 1779. His first guide to the Lakes was written at Titeup Hall.

Black marble records the famous portrait painter, George Romney, who died at Kendal in 1802. Romney was the pupil of Christopher Steele, the portrait artist at premises in Redman's Yard and who, before he went up to London and became famous, could get perhaps £10 for a commission. During the ministry of Dr Symonds the church communion plate was stolen, comprising seven heavy silver pieces, which were never to be recovered, although the wooden box that contained them was brought back years later.

Unofficially the large churchyard was used as a children's playground until enclosed by palisading in 1823. I pictured the bell ringers of early days as strong, enthusiastic fell men for, the story goes, one bell 'burst' and another 'cracked', leading eventually to a mighty peal of ten. Waterloo was celebrated on a new peal increased to eight, supervised by Nicholas Wilson, one of the first scientific bell ringers in the north of England. Kendal church bells became known as one of the most harmonious peals in the kingdom. Mr G. Jennings created a record by assisting, for the fiftieth time, to ring a peal in honour of Queen Victoria's birthday. Some Kendalians, however, objected to the use of church bells for every occasion of merrymaking. Now placed in the belfry of the 80ft tower is a small sanctus bell dated 1537, named 'Tinkler', which was once used to summon boys to the old grammar school next to the church. Another Jennings, John, church sexton for over sixty years, worked with five vicars, ten curates, four organists and four vergers in his time, but Mr Clements is building up a comparable score.

THE ROMANS

The Romans had a settlement earlier than that of the church, developing their fort, Alavna, by utilising the River Kent as a barrier on three sides. Lines of forts and stations were constructed along major routes, the one from Lancaster passing through Watercrook, Concangium. The Kendal-based Roman station, excavated over a century ago in Nicholson's day, yielded coins, broken statues, an altar, urns and bricks from a hypocaust. River flooding uncovered more: an urn of human bones and two skeletons. Dark red stone, used by Roman engineers, found its way into farmhouses; one stone monument erected by 'two freedmen of P. Aelius Bassus' was found at Watercrook and is at present on loan from the British Museum to Kendal Museum. At Watch Field, originally named Wathfield, east of Kendal, the Romans guarded a ford over the Kent. When, in time of plague, one tenth of England's population died, tradition has it that food was left for the Kendalians at Coneybeds, yet another Roman encampment in their system of lookout posts. No one dared to enter or leave the town or travel any distance. Occupation of their stone fort was probably AD 82 to 340 and finds are housed at Kendal Museum, which was once the old warehouse of Whitwell, Hargreaves & Company near the railway.

In June 1987 a Roman coin from the reign of Philip I, dated AD 245, was found by a Kendal schoolgirl on the bank of the river not far from the parish church. Thomas Braithwaite of Burneside Hall collected silver, gold and brass coins, mostly Roman, but discovered none at the Ambleside fort. These were eventually given to Oxford University.

KENDAL CASTLE

The ancient, grey hump of a sprawling castle overlooks both the river and the town, lending a grand style, which few places can match. The power of barons in the

The ruins of Kendal Castle, c. 1870.

Castle dairy.

twelfth century, when each had his castle – and there were 1,115 in Britain – was expressed in their demand for 'white rent', payment in silver. Villeins were drudges, barons' property; small wonder such tyrants assumed ogre status in the folk tales. Gilbert Fitzrenfriend probably built Kendal Castle in the reign of King John, at first as a circular tower but later extended and improved for comfort. There may have been an earlier wooden castle but what remains is of dark blue local rock with window and doorjambs of red sandstone. Equipped with a mill to grind corn and a dairy, it probably had a bridge and portcullis and was approached from Stramongate, the north bridge over Kendal. The century-old photograph on page 37 shows more of the castle than now exists; today's remaining arches are ground-floor storerooms of the manor house with an adjoining tower where the baron and his family lived.

Catherine Parr, born at the castle, the Kendal woman who became a queen of England as sixth wife to Henry VIII, was commended in his will for many virtues and bequeathed £3,000 in gold and jewellery. A religious, dutiful woman (her Book of Devotions is preserved in the town hall), she learned, in spite of her skilful handling of Henry, which probably saved her head, that 'it is a vain thing to trust in a man'.

When William Camden viewed the castle, despite walls of 5ft thickness guarded by three towers, all was in 'a state of dilapidation'. One huge wall blew down in 1824 after which trees were planted, foundations strengthened and walls repaired, as part of Queen Victoria's Jubilee celebrations. Abbot Hall and Park were acquired at the same time.

Changes to the River Kent's banks included the planting of many trees.

The sixth baron who lived at Kendal Castle was one of those present at Runnymede when King John was forced to sign the Magna Carta, which gave even more power to the barons. One apportionment of castle, town and lands reserved Kentmere village for Margaret de Ross's youngest daughter, in whose family it remained until the time of Charles I. Thomas de Ross was baron for sixty-one years, outliving his son, who married into the Strickland family at Sizergh Castle.

STREETS, FAIRS AND MARKETS

Speed's map of Kendale in 1614, with New Biggen, Kent Lane, Free Schole and the Ankeriche is charmingly embellished with a pilgrim, staff in hand, and labourers behind the plough. Kendal was by then one of the best corn markets in the north. An 1832 plan gives more information: Tenter Fell; Miller Close; Friends' School; Sandes Hospital; House of Correction. The gas works and canal had arrived. On market days vast quantities of butter were sold, much of which went to the manufacturing towns, and cartloads of potatoes plus twenty-seven varieties of fish caught on Leven Sands. The right of a weekly market was first granted in 1189. Elizabeth I and Charles I added privileges – two weekly markets and two annual fairs could be held. By special permission – and it is very popular – a market is held on Christmas Eve.

Stricklandgate, associated with 'stirks', is referred to as the Drovers' Road and was the first in Britain to be covered with macadam. It was tested with hard core and broken rocks on behalf of the Cumberland and Westmorland Turnpike Trust, by whom John Macadam was hired.

Before 1909 the Market Place, formerly Mercers' Lane, was enclosed. Town stocks were set up here between the church and Ring o' Bells Inn. A square-towered Moat Hall had remained in use until 1859 and it was a sad day when this historic building was burned down in 1969. With hundreds of today's passers-by not noticing it, at the side of this street is the 'call', 'cold', or 'ca' 'steean', as Westmorland dialect has it, part of an old market cross or, more likely, a remnant of St George's chapel. All public matters were 'called' before the days of the clanging bellman with his roar of 'Oyez'.

History is all around in the crowded streets, especially the 'spine' of Kendal: Kirkland, Stricklandgate and Highgate which, despite so many changes, still have an atmosphere lent by Ye Olde Pharmacy, Farmer's Tea and Coffee Rooms and many old inns. An interesting, carved model of a bristly black boar, the trade sign of the Black Bull Brush factory, and the Kendal Mint Cake works of J.E. Wilson are close to Sricklandgate. Of two famous inns – The Woolpack and The King's Arms – there

Kendal from the castle, 1902. On the north slope of Kendal Fell, close to the Serpentine Woods is an 'alpine' meadow, from which fine views of the River Kent can be seen.

exists a painting of the latter depicting coaching days where now Marks and Spencer reign. Robert Stirzaker's painting in the town hall shows the Kendal to Liverpool coach, Telegraph.

James I and Bonnie Prince Charlie both stayed in houses on Stricklandgate, the second main street where once was the House of Correction. The main street, originally Soutergate (shoemaker's street), is now Highgate, once separated from Stricklandgate by a large building, Newbiggin ('biggin' means cottage), made of wood, with a row of shops at street level and the second floor overhanging just as on Christmas card versions. It was pulled down in 1803. I noticed that the printers, Titus Wilson's premises, have been acquired by Arrowcroft Group plc for development and hoped that the Midland Bank, corseted in scaffolding, would care for the stone lion on its roof.

The eighteenth-century yards, a feature of Kendal, giving access to the River Kent for tanning, dyeing, washing, and of which Dr Manning's Yard has been preserved, emphasise how great a part the river played in the life of the town. Dr Manning's, previously Braithwaite's Yard, was the site of a drysalters and dyestuffs business. Others are Elephant Yard, White Horse Yard and Blackhall Yard. These mysterious ginnels snaking off the streets' roar of traffic and the arches leading to the Mews are reminiscent of Edinburgh's Royal Mile.

Finkle Street, which contained the New Shambles (Watts Lane), is now a pleasant oasis in which to buy gifts and flowers and slopes gently to the river with a fine view out to the fellside. The Old Shambles on the west side is said to have been the scene of the slaughter of 1,700 beasts carried out in the street, which would have made it offensively smelly and gruesome.

Long ago, milkmaids and young men danced around the Maypole; the men to celebrate completion of their long apprenticeships. Workmen dug up its stone base in Kirkland when laying pipes. Every twenty-one years a Guild was held but the last one, celebrated between 4 and 6 June 1759, so impoverished some tradesmen by its extravagance that the practice was discontinued. 'Taylors, shearmen-dyers, wool combers, weavers, shoemakers, ironmongers and mettlemen, tanners, builders, mercers, glovers and skinners' all took part in the processions.

Whether any were forced into the workhouse where 'the poor were not to be maintained in idleness' I do not know, but profits from their labour (workhouse inmates manufactured Harden, a coarse sacking made from flax) averaged over £1,000 a year during which 53,000 yards were produced.

Thomas Sandes, who made a great deal of money from selling Kendal cottons, founded Sandes Hospital and School, the elegant building on Highgate, which was gifted to the town by Thomas and Catherine Sandes, as shown by the initialled crest. Some forty-three charities provided for children and widows, dating from 1561 when the first, Gilpin's Rents, was set up. Henry Parke's Gift bestowed '74 pounds in cloth for the Poor'. A board in the parish church lists 'Donations to the Poor for Bread', all of which lead thoughts naturally to Kendal's main source of wealth.

But firstly I must say a word about the inns. These tell the story of what must have been a thirsty town on market days and maybe still is: Shakespeare; Bowman

Nether Bridge, Kendal.

Highgate; Cock and Dolphin (by Nether Bridge); Ye Olde Fleece Inn; Queen's; Seven Stars; Dun Horse; George and Dragon; The Woolpack, dated 1781. Oh for the original inn signs which ran to life-size carvings instead of the adequate but insipid versions of today!

KENDAL GREEN

On hearing the 'murmuring noyse' of the River Kent on his approach from Shap, Lieutenant Hammond, an eighteenth-century military man from Norwich, observed that: 'the town is like a windmill saile, centre for cloth manufacturer, the surrounding fields are covered with cloth stretched out on tenters to dry'. It resembled a biblical fuller's field I should think, especially as washing was also brought down from fellside to river, later still to the public washing house, to hang, drying on banks and bushes.

In rhyme with this chapter heading, Michael Drayton goes on: 'for making of our cloth scarce matched in all the land', and there you have it. Worn by Kendal bowmen or on the field at Flodden and made reference to by none other than William Shakespeare, Kendal green cloth was renowned.

Liverpool Custom House figures show how much was exported: 4,000 pieces of Kendal Green went to America and 2,693 pieces to Virginia. Kendal cottons were also much in demand in Barbados. Spinning and fulling, at first done in the houses, progressed to mills equipped with great beating hammers. Along the shores of the Kent, Mint and Sprint were hundreds of tenters, men who fixed the cloth on frames by tenterhooks and kept a sharp eye on the weather. Early cloth was of poor quality; it was the development of fulling and dyeing processes and the influence of Flemish weavers that made Kendalmen famous for their cloth, leading to the town's motto 'Wool is my Bread'.

True Kendal Green, the much-prized deep shade, was prepared from vegetable dyes, using gorse and whinberry from the fells and potash from burned bracken, although in Kentmere I heard that the dye was produced from small yellow flowers picked on the marsh, the second process being a dip in blue dye.

Cloth was carried in long packhorse trains before covered wagons were used. Four times a week a forty-horse train wound its way to the Westmorland port of Milnthorpe. 'Everybody is knitting', wrote Daniel Defoe in his journal when he visited Kendal. Again, raw wool was carried out to the homesteads in Kentmere, Dentdale and their surroundings, to be collected later as hosiery. E.W. Thompson & Sons, still producing top quality woollen socks, started business in Kendal in 1878, but the industry itself dates from the seventeenth century. A grey stone building, '1897 Hosiery Works', is to be seen not far from the railway station.

From socks to shoes brings in K Shoemakers Ltd, later owned by Clarks. It originated at Robert Somervell's leather shop in about 1840, where he was aided by his brother in making shoes completely by hand until American sewing machines were brought in. Some idea of this industry, is indicated by the presence of sixty tanners in the last Guild procession.

Gawith Hoggarth & Company's celebrated brown snuff is still made today at Stone Mill, Helsington, where once Faireys had a 'chimney piece and monument factory', handling marble. Tobacco was imported from Maryland to Whitehaven and Maryport while Kendal cottons were exported by return.

Before halfpennies were minted some well-established tradesmen had tokens in use in exchange for goods, struck in their individual design from copper or tin, giving rise to the northern term 'brass', indicative of wealth.

RAILWAYS AND BRIDGES

In 1846 the Kendal to Windermere railway opened. Today's County Hotel, with its Catherine Parr bar, was once the Railway Hotel opposite the station. Nicknamed 'Kendal Tommy', a small branch line train, consisting of a Furness red tank engine and two carriages, ran from Grant to Arnside, Sandside, Heversham and Hincaster to Kendal. To keep passengers warm in winter, long oval cylinders called 'foot warmers' were pushed into the compartments just before the train set off. It was reported in the Westmorland Gazette on 13 February 1841 that 'there was some sighing for the old coaching days when the mail train was three hours and ten minutes late from Preston; owing to rain freezing on the rails the wheels could not bite'.

As more and more people visited the Lake District, takings at the toll houses had increased. Netherfield Toll House near Natland took £377 in 1812, which was not long after the Turnpike Trusts were inaugurated. The Kendal to Milnthorpe road was turnpiked in 1759, and Greenodd to Levens in 1820.

The first all-stone bridge was built in 1743. Millers Close Bridge had to go when the Lancaster and Kendal canal came, but it was rebuilt later. Kent Lane was widened, more paving done, more houses built of limestone from Kendal Fell and large warehouses appeared at Canal Basin.

Modern Kendal

The 'chattering river', the Mint, passes through Grayrigg to join the Kent at Mintsfleet where a thriving industrial estate has grown up. Like the Kent and Sprint, the Mint and its mill walks were pounded by the feet of workmen handling rolls of cloth, for which mill rents were payable. In the face of modern industry Kendal has not stood still but has welcomed insurance, carpets, hornware, turbines and the continuance of shoes, socks and the famous Kendal Mint Cake. As the focal point of the region, there is much going on and Kendal is well served culturally. Abbot Hall,

A view of Kendal in the 1980s.

once the town house of the Wilson family of Dallam Tower, lies north of the parish church. As the name implies, it was once the abbot's residence when he visited from the Abbey of St Mary's in York. Today's beautifully proportioned Georgian house, in its pleasant setting by the river, has a fine collection of paintings by artists of such standing as Romney and Ruskin and furniture by Gillows of Lancaster. We found the small car park near Abbot Hall convenient for everything, including the pleasant riverside walk in both directions and the climbs to Serpentine Woods and the castle. Abbot Hall has been designated one of forty venues in the country for major exhibitions. In 1987 one notable exhibition was the work of the exiled German artist, Kurt Schwitters, who died in Kendal in 1948 and was world famous for his collage pictures.

The Museum of Lakeland Life and Industry, also housed at Abbot Hall, recaptured the life of an area in its trades, crafts and farms. In 1973 it was awarded Museum of the Year when that prize was offered for the first time. Another accolade-winner is Kendal Museum of Natural History and Archaeology. Displays trace the archaeology of the region from the Stone Age onwards and reflect a town proud of its history and working hard to conserve it.

The Brewery Arts Centre, set high, close to the heart of the town and opened in 1971, has a unique home – a 150-year-old brewery, itself an interesting item of industrial archaeology. Extensively converted to become the liveliest arts complex in the north, it combines an extensive range of facilities, each year holding the Kendal Jazz Festival and the Kendal Folk Festival when international stars shine. The work of the Pocket Theatre allows groups of actors to take productions around Cumbrian villages and to perform in schools and clubs. There is recreation and enjoyment throughout the seasons at this gateway to the Lakes.

All this activity, on a firm basis of long history, continues to be reported in the Westmorland Gazette, which was established in 1918. Although concentrating on the present, it too has an interesting past. Originally the newspaper was launched with the help of the Lowther family and William Wordsworth to boost their man fighting the Liberal candidate in the general election. Its most distinguished, though short-lived, editor was Thomas de Quincey, who left within a year. The Lowthers at that time preferred slander to literary genius.

Special events in such a magnetic tourist area are legion; Cumbria Steam Gathering; Kendal Folk Festival; Kendal Jazz Festival, and the two-week Kendal Gathering ending with a Torchlight Parade in September. Here truly is a town throbbing with life.

4

'Winds Somewhere Safe to Sea'

'Even the weariest river', wrote Algernon Charles Swinburne, 'winds somewhere safe to sea.' At no point did we think the River Kent weary, but it seemed tame one showery April day, flowing beneath the three massive stone arches of Stramongate Bridge. However, historic flood levels in 1831 (when the population was 11,037), 1861, 1898, 1927 and 1954 are recorded nearby on green slate giving this lie, which awakens speculation as to how often the wayward Kent has flowed into the Bridge Hotel. Cornelius Nicholson, FGS, FSA, Justice of the Peace and a Deputy Lieutenant, who married a Kendal girl, would have approved of the Flood Relief System of 1972 to 1978, for he loved the 'auld grey town' and chose to be

Rigg's Coaches. In the nineteenth century these coaches ran from Rigg's Windermere Hotel, by the drinking fountain, which was later moved to the Brewery Arts Centre, Kendal. Fares were 7s and 'one third extra on top' where nine sat with the driver, luggage in between.

Westmorland Brass band, 1890.

buried there. Having visited the Museum of Lakeland Life and Industry we found ourselves nibbling an after dinner treat from the firm established in 1840, Quiggin's Kendal Mint Cake, in company with numerous mallard. Besides blacksmiths, wheelwrights, bobbin makers, coopers, printers, brewers, all bringing skills, it was shown without doubt that the weavers established Kendal as England's pioneer town in the wool industry, a status that continued for 600 years. What had been processes in the trade – chapman, webster, bowker, cropper, shearman – passed into usage, along with others, as proper names.

The days on which we covered the lower reaches of the river were also in April, a cold spring sharpened with the rawness of generous rain showers. Swollen by heavy rains and melted snows, the Kent was then spectacular. As we approached through National Trust Brigsteer Woods, where the tiny golden wild daffodils, wood anemones and celandine bloomed, there was no one about, but all around a sense of quickening life: clear bird calls; tangled brambles disturbed by robin and wren; wild garlic pushing greenly through beech mast; the scents of soaked earth; and the delicate tracery of saplings. Another month and the misty haze of bluebells would cover the heart of the woods where now shrivelled, brown leaves clung, those few left by gales that had torn branches from looming trunks. Ivy, holly, vivid green moss and the bright silver of birch, lighting a grey day, were also present.

We caught sight of Scout Scar and Lord's Plain, with Lyth Valley beyond, as we drove past woods and villages. Cottage gardens, along the narrow, hilly road passing

Park End Farm, Honeybee House, Wheatsheaf Hotel, Field End Farm and Plum Tree Farm, were awash with colours: tulips, primulas, daffodils and large cushions of purple aubretia; it is a road that was once a packhorse route between Kendal and Ulverston, traversed in 1811 by John Clarke, 'Kendal and Ulverston carrier'.

Not far from Prizet we noticed another interesting name, Helsington Laithes, going back to Norse origins, 'hlatha' meaning barn. Provender gathered from the fertile valley floor was no doubt stored here. Sir Thomas Seymour stayed at Helsington Laithes Manor House when he unsuccessfully paid court to Catherine Parr, who was then living at Sizergh Castle.

NATLAND

The river at Hawes Bridge came roaring down, tracking through its worn, limestone base as we stopped short of Natland. Nailed onto trees were Kent Angling Association notices forbidding canoeing, which would indeed have been fraught amid such a churning current dragging with it all that came its way. We found a small ruin, which might have been a mill. Henry Hoggarth built snuff mills on the Mint and on the Kent at Natland, sending his product all over the world.

Natland was the best-kept village in South Lakeland that year. St Mark's church stands on spacious Natland village green and was completed in 1910 by the busy pair of Lancaster architects, Paley and Austin. It is the fourth to stand there, the

Egg Tommy's home was near to this spot by the River Kent, Natland, seen here in summer 1987.

earliest being built in 1246. Many chapels of ease were set up in the large parish of Kendal, but all baptisms, weddings and funerals had to take place at Kendal parish church. Especially in a mountainous area, burial in winter was difficult, a well nigh impossible task, and recognised 'dead roads', the easiest routes, were trodden. As at Kentmere, church registers date from the 1770s. Along Helm Lane on the south side of the church, Natland Abbey, reputed to be a grange of St Mary's Abbey, is passed on the left, then High House with its seventeenth-century chimneys. From here Helm Common is reached and 'back of Helm' giving views of the Howgill Fells. By the Wishing Tree hundreds of pebbles have been pushed into the wall, representing the secret yearnings of passers-by. Inviting 'areas off' are to Crosscrake, Endmoor and Well Ends Lane. We photographed a handsome barn with low walls, long, pitched roof and stone balls ornamenting gable ends: a classic example of these parts. We made for the Trig sign, our destination, the summit of Helm, once the site of an Iron Age fort and Roman lookout point. One of the finest views of the Kent area is obtained from here, showing the loop of the river, the site of Agricola's camp, Alvana, in AD 70, at Watercrook. This important part of the Kent valley has for centuries been a focal point. The Scandinavian settlers who followed the Anglians may have built a temple in Natland to their pagan god Nati. The 'crosse in Natland' is mentioned in 1312, as is the medieval tithe barn.

This tiny community was transformed by the coming of the railway and it is interesting to note that the Lancaster stone that went into the present church came by canal barge to Hawes Bridge and the Darley Dale stone for dressings, by train.

SEDGWICK

Drifts of daffodils, pussy willow and primroses decorating the high canal embankment greeted us in this clean and charming village, from where you can walk down to the Kent and along the east side of the river to Hawes Bridge. A massive stone bridge, allowing 9ft 6in clearance for traffic, has a long flight of stone steps to the left that, once climbed, reveal the dried-up bed of the canal. Along this canal towpath is a good 1½-mile walk, passing through Larkrigg Wood. This section of the canal, opened in 1796, and linking with Kendal in 1819, served the gunpowder mill run by the successful Quaker family, Wakefields, who lived at Sedgwick House, now a Lancashire Education Special School. Mary Wakefield, a singer of international repute, founded the Westmorland Music Festival that, in its time, has featured such famous names as Dame Clara Butt and Malcolm Sargent. Her great-grandfather, John, founded a bank in Kendal. Mary was born in Stricklandgate but her father built a house at Prizet prior to inheriting Sedgwick House, the complete rebuilding and refurbishing of which he entrusted to Paley and Austin.

Near Sedgwick, where there is a new bridge, the Kent continued its headlong course, gushing over the fissured limestone flats to speed under yet another bridge, over another crashing weir and then suddenly to be divided by an island. Here I found the most beautiful of flowers, a whole clump of water avens. 'Aven' means river. Add to the list, bog primroses at Skelsmergh; stonecrop on Tenter Fell; wild

Workers' cottages, Old Row, Sedgwick.

angelica in Longsleddale; and yellow poppy in Natland, where celandine and later red bladder campion and rose bay willow herb were common. As summer advances, yellow sow thistle, ragwort and miles of Queen Anne's Lace grow by the roadside, flowers and leaves hang heavy with drops of dew and intertwine with purple vetch and orchis growing alongside a very busy road.

THE LANCASTER TO KENDAL CANAL

As we toured the area there were many reminders of canals in the shape of low, graceful, stone bridges. The opening of the Lancaster to Kendal Canal brought more prosperity and led to appropriate improvements in Kendal. On the anniversary of Waterloo in 1819 a grand aquatic procession, consisting of a decorated barge, fifteen smaller boats, flags everywhere and music from three bands, wound down the new canal. The party joined up at Crooklands and, as they neared Kendal, the boom of cannon from Castle Hill sounded. The passengers of 'the packets', which arrived in the canal basin at 4 p.m., went to 'a sumptuous dinner and a ball at the King's Arms attended by 120 persons'.

Building the canal revived the brick trade; clay deposits at Moss Side Farm supplied the raw material for making bricks used in the construction of bridges and Hincaster tunnel (through which canal boats had to be poled), and provided employment for 100 men and thirty horses.

The Preston to Kendal Canal, down which damsons were transported, opened in 1820 with the swift packet boat Water Witch that 'commenced running daily on the canal, leaving Kendal at 6 a.m. and reaching Prestion at 1 p.m. . . . arriving back at Kendal at 8.45 p.m.' Trotting horses pulled the barges along at the rate of 8 miles an hour and were much more amenable in nature than the 'navvies' who had worked on the canal's construction and were often so pugnacious that they were locked up near Milnthorpe Market Cross.

SIZERGH CASTLE

From Hincaster, which may have been a Roman camp, is a sudden view of Sizergh Castle. A line of willows whitening in the wind and the delicate yellow stars of low-growing silver weed provide vivid memories of the day we went to Sizergh and Levens, conveniently visited as an important pair. The imposing castle, originally a pele tower, has been the home of the Strickland family since 1239 when Sir William de Stirklande married the heiress of the Sizergh estate. Sir Thomas Strickland fought at the Battle of Agincourt and during the Civil War the family remained staunchly loyal to the Stuarts, seeking exile in France in 1688. Many treasures date from the time when they were supported by the French royal family; Lady Strickland acted as governess within the court circle.

Sizergh Castle.

It takes a good few hours to explore the grounds and castle. I particularly liked the massive carved wood screen, dated 1558, placed some years ago in the Great Hall. Before that, coaches and carriages drove right through and out the other side under the high, studded doors, depositing travellers at the foot of the staircase leading into the pele tower, which is situated west of the river. There is of course a splendid view of the Kent, the higher one goes up the tower, and a strong sense of medieval days, not least from the thick oak planks bearing marks of the adze applied by hands from centuries back.

Alongside the castle, bordering beautiful grounds (the rock and water gardens made of local limestone are internationally famous) is a very large grassed area, formerly a tilt yard. All around are views of rolling Westmorland county and we were fortunate enough to meet the head gardener who led us to a magnificent lavender-coloured lace cap hydrangea, the grey stone walls of the castle beings its perfect setting. One of the Lord's tenants, in 1872, Mr C. Garnett of Low Sizergh Farm, was the winner of ploughing matches as far away as Lancaster.

LEVENS HALL

Mentioned in the Domesday Book as Lefuens, the village was once called Beathwaite Green, where a number of very poor peat cutters and their children lived. The peat carts brought their turf loads over limestone hillsides, Helsington Barrows, Scot Scar, Brigsteer, Witherslack Quaggs and Foulshaw Mosses. 'Ten a penny as

Levens Hall and topiary gardens.

long as we've any,' was their cry all the way to Kendal. Mary Howard of Levens, who started the Howard Orphan Home, educated the children, who ran barefoot and lived in miserable cottages.

A happy, whole day can be spent at Levens Hall, especially if the weather is good and, for a wonder, it was. We chose a rare pearl from that wet summer of 1987. The deer park, one of the oldest remaining in England, running by the River Kent; the ancient topiary garden laid out by the French gardener Monsieur Beaumont, who trained at Versailles; the house itself, another pele tower, are all sheer delight. Owned by the de Redmans, the Bellinghams and now the Bagot family, Levens, like Sizergh, is steeped in history. 'Luck to Levens while the Kent flows' is the traditional toast, always drunk in wine from the estate's brewhouse.

Of many treasures there is the Constable glass from which the famous 'Morocco' was drunk. It is 16½in high and 4½in across and engraved 'Levens High Constable'. After proclaiming the fair at Milnthorpe open on 12 May it was customary for the mayor and the Corporation of Kendal to move on to Levens. A feast of radishes, laver bread, butter, cheese and the strong ale that was kept twenty years before tapping and which newcomers had to 'down in one', was laid before hundreds, the radishes being wheeled up in barrow loads.

Tom Longmire, champion wrestler of England, appeared at Levens athletic sports in 1899, a feature of the Levens feast. Cricket matches were held, sometimes beside the Kent at Ninezergh Farm, Captain Bagot's cricket XI being drawn from family and tenants. Bowls was also popular, as is revealed in Henry Bellingham's diary. Newspapers show that 'the sports of the country people celebrating Nelson's Battle of Trafalgar victory' involved 'a leg of mutton and a gallon of porter to the winner of 100 yards in sacks'. There was 'a good hat to be wrestled for, a pig prize to anyone who catches him by the tail, a Michaelmas Day goose, a cheese to be rolled down hill, the prize to whoever stops it, a pound of tobacco to be grinned for and a round of beef for the best cricketer'.

It was traditional for countrymen to breed poultry for cockfighting in the Kent area before it was, like bull-baiting, banned in 1835. It was a favourite pastime among the boys of Heversham School, where the master received gratuities on Shrove Tuesday in the form of 'cock pennies'. Even some clergymen indulged and in Westmorland, Cumberland and Lancashire the tradition continued in secret. Of many romantic stories attached to Levens, one tells of a gypsy, turned away on the point of starvation. She cursed the house, declaring that no male heir would be born until the River Kent ran dry. The birth of a boy in 1896 when the river froze solid coincided with that of a white stag from the herd, another Levens omen signalling change of fortune.

HEVERSHAM

Climbing Heversham Head, 400ft high, we came across a herd of bullocks, possible adversaries; however this time they came 'not single spies but battalions'. It was quite easy to outflank them by following the churchyard wall and skirting the wood. To gaze on a glorious June day over such a panorama of bay, estuary, Bowland Fells, Farleton Knott, Arnside Knott, Cartmel Fells, was worth the effort.

Heversham became part of the Levens Estate in 1597, bought by James Bellingham. But its beginnings as an Anglian settlement go back to the seventh century, when Haefar sailed up to establish his farm by the church. In the sixteenth and seventeenth centuries the tides of the Kent estuary flowed over the mosses to the foot of Heversham village itself. The name Fluster Gate derives from local farmers hurriedly having to head their sheep away from advancing waters. The beams in Bank Farm are said to have come from a wrecked ship, and Haverflatts, near the track of the old railway, may be an ancient settlement.

Prince's Way now bypasses the village east of the Kent estuary, referred to as Evresham in the Domesday Book. We passed the famous old school house and the site of the cockpit, both of which are the subject of a book. The old Ship Inn was adapted to become the headmaster's house. Daily from his hearth, smouldering

Heversham Old School.

peats, for which the boys contributed peat money, were carried up for the school fire. The peat-burning fires of Kentmere were never allowed to go out from one year to another. A very old custom was that when moving from a farm, you transported your peat fire in a bucket to the new homestead. When Edward Wilson founded the grammar school at Heversham in 1613 he set in motion a great record of academic achievement. 'A galaxy of famous old boys', including Ephraim Chambers, is recalled in R.D. Humber's interesting history, which began in this small limestone building with its typical Westmorland round chimneys.

A cross shaft in Heversham church porch, designed with animals, birds and scrolls, may indicate the presence of an eighth-century monastery. Westmorland's oldest recorded church was burned down in 1601 because of a careless workman. 'Ornaments, books, monuments, chests, organs, bells and all things perished' but a staggering parish chest about ten feet long, of heavy, adze-marked oak, fitted with iron straps, can be seen today, perhaps the only item to escape the flames.

Heversham parish was once one of the biggest in the country, covering 20,000 acres of the lower Kent valley. It was an ancient parish, having direct links with the Lake District and extending up to two miles off Lake Windermere's eastern shore. The ram's head on a church pillar denotes a community given over to agriculture. One headstone in the churchyard, which is also remarkable for splendid horse chestnut trees, records Jane, the wife of Henry Swinglehurst, who sailed round Cape Horn with three children in 1855 and, after visiting the coast of Peru, returned to Hincaster House in 1859 with her husband and five children.

The Blue Bell Inn, in 1898, in the days when it had a smithy next door, sold ale drawn from the wood at twopence a pint. Here were stabled carriages and horses of the gentry while they were in church. Another familiar sight was the long line of horses pulling carts laden with damsons at fruit picking time. On our run through the Lyth Valley that year we could not buy a single damson.

'Beware of possible bulls' along the riverside from College Green to Fishcarling Head warned Kendal Deanery Walks, so we gave it a miss. It was the end of a day when the Bay was aflame with one of those incomparable red-gold sunsets. Pleasantly tired, we turned for home. I was sleepily thinking that the odd bull would have meant nothing to Jane Swinglehurst.

PELE TOWERS

This chapter should close with a note about the pele towers, built as defences against the Scots and other fierce neighbours. Some merged later into mansions like Sizergh and Levens or farms like Wraysholme and Kentmere Hall. There were fortress pele towers like Dallam, guarding the estuary, but most stemmed from the border wars between the English and Scots. The Union of 1603, when James I succeeded to the throne of England, was an attempt to end the strife. Sizergh's pele tower is the largest in Cumbria and dates from Edward III's reign. When the warning rang out, the baron, his family, tenants, cattle and sheep all crowded into these strong fortifications. Of 8,350 archers supplied for the border wars in 1584, Westmorland sent 4,142. When the Scots burned Kendal they 'put all inhabitants to the sword, sparing neither age nor sex'. The record of one foray itemises 192 towns burned, 403 Scots slain and 10,000 horned cattle, 200 goats and 12,000 sheep stolen.

The second floor of the pele tower at Sizergh, with its adze-hewn floorboards and fifteenth-century window, was where the lord and his men lived, alert for a signal from the top floor where a constant lookout must have been kept towards the high fells. Whinfell beacon, 1,544ft above sea level, was one of the places from which warning of a raid could be given. Edward Ayray, in 1543, is listed as one of Walter Strickland's Sizergh tenants at arms. The Aireys figure in tax lists for Kentmere in 1332, the Ruckes from Skelsmergh in the 1500s. River Kent area surnames, the spelling of which have undergone many changes, have been in use for close on a millennium, figuring in Farrer's Records of Kendale.

Kentmere – an ancient ruin in a Kentdale lane.

5

'On Either Side the River Lie...'

EAST SIDE

This chapter evolved slowly, the product of many miles covered over many months, for it was a pleasurable necessity to explore both sides of the estuary and to go back for what we had missed, plotting as we went more townships and villages on our map. Taking the east side first and remembering that the River Kent has now wound 'safe to sea', we commenced at Milnthorpe, which once had important maritime connections, then moved down the estuary as far as Jenny Brown's Point.

The birds of the fells and meadows, kestrel, raven, buzzard, magpie, martin and pipit, although we saw the last-mentioned on peat mosses under Whitbarrow, give place to oyster catcher known locally as sea-pie, ringed plover and herring gulls in their hundreds. March's violent moods tossed black-headed gulls about like confetti as they gathered on flooded pastures. There was the sound of a bittern at Silverdale, possibly strayed from Leighton Moss and, nesting in mind, the sight of intelligent jackdaws helping themselves to wool from the backs of Rough Fell sheep. Grey geese and pink-footed geese arrive in autumn, flying up the estuary to rich feeding grounds of arthropods and other sea creatures at Grange-over-Sands and Kents Bank. Spring is another good time for bird watching here, binoculars at the ready, with the appearance of grey skua, dunlin, turnstone and godwit. This wide panorama of estuary comes in salty contrast to moorland heights and the lush wetness of rich parkland like Levens. Morecambe Bay has a large nesting population, which a much bickered-over Barrage would sadly disturb, robbing the infinite sandflats, a shield of burnished silver for 120 miles, of their incomparable atmosphere. The delicate interplay between tawny sand, chocolate mud, tussocky mossland, and sun, cloud, sky and water would be interfered with in an area made glowing or mysteriously hazy at the caprice of weather.

Early immigrants, missionaries like St Patrick, marauders, Angles and Norsemen entered the bay, eyeing the river mouths, wooded shelter, rich pastures, wild life on the mosses and good dry points, all with the creation of settlement in mind. David Pownall graphically describes Morecambe Bay as 'a vast restaurant with millions of small animals on the menu'. Certainly fishing and farming have been a way of life for centuries where Rivers Kent, Keer and Leven ebb and flow. At some period, according to Thomas West's Antiquities of Furness, Leven and Kent sands were covered with woods. Excavation in the eighteenth century revealed large trees in riverbeds and mossland in pits, which people dug up to use as fertiliser.

Of many cargoes the saddest must surely have been the little black boys brought across from Liverpool, smuggled up the River Leven to Windermere and landed at Storrs Hall by Colonel John Bolton, to be hidden and subsequently sold as house-boys for Lake District mansions.

MILNTHORPE

This ancient town, situated on the north bank of the River Bela, is referred to in a Heversham church book of accounts as Millthrop. 'For the first time, the town of Millthrop in Westmorland is named Milnthorp', reported the *Lancaster Gazette* on 10 December 1832. The River Bela joins the Kent estuary opposite Whitebarrow Scar, the 'white hill', where once the great white-tailed sea eagle had its nest. The Kent, being navigable as far as the Bela, small ships of 20 tons burden could moor. Harbour dues belonged to the House of Levens. The Custom House is now the dairy in Park Road, and this little port, the only one in Westmorland, had links all over the world. Ships sailed up at high water to moor opposite Dallam Tower, goods being lowered over the vessels' sides into carts. In the eighteenth century salt and coal were handled. Pig iron was brought from Scotland to be beaten at Sedgwick forge and sent off again with gunpowder, slate, leather and other products from the little mills along the Bela and Kent. Mention has already been made of cloth. The ships Kent, Isabella and Slack sailed to Liverpool, returning with wood, trays, clothes and useful items for the pedlars' packs. The coming of the railway and the making of the Kendal and Lancaster canal hastened the end of the port, as indeed it did that of other calling places in the estuary, but when Milnthorpe prospered Daniel Wilson employed men to rebuild Dallam Tower. An imposing porch with four Tuscan columns was added in 1826, further enhancing the deer park, rookery and famous heronry where Thomas Gough of Arnside counted twenty herons' nests in 1877. On one occasion we actually saw a whole herd of deer close to the road: a very beautiful sight. Mount's 1826 map shows a paper and a flax mill on the 'Beela' that, sixty years later, were making twine and sacking, eventually to become John Dobson's comb factory. As a site of industry, it dates back to the eighth century and Anglian settlement, but with the coming of steam, water mills were usurped.

Milnthorpe was a market town, which for years had a corn market, regular Sunday hiring fairs and spring and autumn cattle fairs, the last being in 1917. With rights dating back to 1280 there was a staging post with nine inns, a large malt kiln and ropewalks. The town filled to overflowing on market days when Mackereth's worm balls for horses and Hepworth's sheep rot paste found ready buyers; twenty apples cost a penny. Ploughing competitions were held in Paradise Fell Field, Ackenthwaite, with its smithy. Surrounded by fresh-water springs, Milnthorpe was ideal for early settlement, but piped water did not arrive until 1908.

Another ancient settlement was at Haverbank in Dallam Park where shore access led to trouble with the squire. The father of novelist Constance Holme was agent for the Wilsons of Dallam Tower and the family lived by the River Bela. These surroundings from youth must have nurtured her considerable talent. Her most famous novel, *The Lonely Plough*, tells of the flood disaster on 16 March 1907, when the Kent's devastating tidal bore swept inland. Between College Green and Halforth farms is Waterside, on the bank of the Kent. This cottage, called Beautiful End in her book, was built in Elizabeth I's reign by Captain John Todd, who sailed into Milnthorpe port and, on retiring from the sea, bought twenty acres of mossland. His descendants have lived at Waterside ever since. In February 1903, a 130-mph gust of wind blew a train off the Leven viaduct. This, the breaching of Brogden's sea wall at Meathop, the carrying away of a haystack by the flood, 'the fury and passion of that tempest', all come out in her books, which show much the same understanding and humanity as the works of Margaret Cropper. She died at Arnside in 1955.

Exactly 100 years back from our July 1987 visit, the death was announced of a Milnthorpe man, John Taylor, who had become head of the Mormon church in Canada. 'His north country perseverance stood him in good stead,' as did that of Pippa Manby-Davis, daughter of a Milnthorpe couple, when she established a world record in 1987, completing 832 miles in the third annual Sri Chinmoy 1,300 mile race. Pippa grew up on Cartmel Fell.

SANDSIDE

A sloop of 100 tons burden saved Thomas North's horse and cart as he was crossing the sands in 1824. This indicates the size of vessel that came 'carrying coal up to Milnthorpe', but the latter had to give way to Dixie's and Sandside, which had wharves for vessels bringing flax and farm produce from Northern Ireland. Coasting vessels brought flour, sugar, cotton, wheat, iron, wines, and took out sacking, twine, sailcloth and hempen cloth from Kendal. Coal and slate came from the Cumberland coast. Trade between Liverpool and Sandside needed twenty-five horses to help unload cargoes.

Carriage of goods inland was improved by a turnpike road from Birkett's Farm, but a time came when ships could no longer sail on the tide. The coming of the

The railway viaduct at Arnside.

The River Kent at Sandside.

railway killed sea traffic, with the Furness railway viaduct over the Kent estuary from Arnside to Grange. Sandside became a holiday resort. Six trippers from Oldham were drowned in 1910, caught by the tidal surge. River Kent men, volunteers in the Boer War, marched from Sandside station to be presented with gold watches. The station stood intact until 1965 but has now gone, like that of Heversham.

Today the Ship Inn, Sandside Garage and a block of flats mainly for the elderly retired look out onto a blank estuary, alongside a few small industries – wood turning, building and joinery. Next to the Cottage Restaurant I noticed an interesting datestone: T.I.A. 1728. A remarkable abundance of salmon was reported here and fishing for fluke was common in the September of 1842. 'In the Kent at Lune', and in the following year, 'an enormous quantity of salmon selling at low prices, Monday ninety-five fish, Tuesday 900 pounds caught, Wednesday 500 pounds caught.'

Leaving healthy and quiet Sandside on a mouth-watering note, we passed on to the wooded area of Storth, high above the shores of the estuary near to what was known as Bomershire Bay, Sandside's best anchorage. The thatched, wattle and daub cottages have all gone, but the Fairy Steps and Hazelslack Tower are what most people come to see. If you can reach the source of the Kent you can get up those 'steps', but it does require caution. Smooth limestone is slippery when wet.

From Storth village we passed All Saints' church, formerly the village wash house, and on to Four Lane Ends. Eventually a muddy footpath through woods passes the ancient pele tower. Before Arnside had a church, worshippers made their way to

Beetham church, up the Fairy Steps which on one visit, seeing the signpost as we approached from the small car park off the busy main road, there came a marvellous view of the Lake District mountains, Furness coast and Kent estuary. The whole of Morecambe Bay beyond was our reward.

ARNSIDE

In an area of what is undeniably unique and 'outstanding beauty' the ANOB Landscape Trust was launched on 20 September 1986, enlisting local people in the future enhancement and conservation of Arnside and Silverdale. In order to protect the fragile, natural structure and resolve conflicts of interest between those who live in the countryside and those who use it for recreation, a three-year venture in countryside management was put under way. Urgency of action grows yearly; witness the proposal to keep motorcars out of the Lake District and for a tourist tax, to repair the decay and erosion caused by thousands of tramping feet. This balance between access and conservation remains at the top of the National Trust aims and the River Kent area is very much a part of it.

Arneside was a small port and shipbuilding centre in the nineteenth century with Hope and Resolution calling for salt. The sloop Leighton was specially built for carrying iron and slate, the Backbarrow Iron Company shipping a furnace to Arnside, which handled hoops, marble, coal and gunpowder among its cargoes.

A ruined pele tower, Arnside.

Captain Bush, master mariner residing at Ye Olde Fighting Cocks Inn, was a customs officer listed in the 1849 Directory where we also find 'Francis John Crossfield, boatbuilder'. Crossfields built hundreds of prawners and yachts. In the 1880s, 150 fishing boats swept Morecambe Bay, dwindling to about seventy-five in 1930. Now there are fewer than a dozen. Keen yachtsmen restore Crossfield's craft: Nora; Juanita; Ploughboy; Frances Louise; because they are famed for their beautiful underwater lines and designed for speed. The customs warehouse is now the headquarters of Arnside Sailing Club, which arranges small yacht races to Fleetwood and Barrow. Underhill and Underwood look like limestone coastguard cottages from the 1850s. In 1760, Arnside had been a fishing village with twenty-three dwellings but, a century later, Bulmer's Directory describes the beach as 'covered one hour with ships another with pedestrians', giving some idea of the speed of the tidal bore sweeping from the bay. A warning siren is sounded. At about the same time efforts were made to form a mussel bed, by the fishermen scattering fifty bags of mussels, hoping for propagation. 'The best and largest were caught near Holme Island in 1862', reported the *Westmorland Gazette*.

The Kent Viaduct

It was the silting of the estuary and the coming of the railway that finished Arnside's sea traffic and also the Cross Sands route as a highroad. The Ulverston and Lancaster railway viaduct was constructed between July 1856 and 1857 on the line of an old ford over the river, a very difficult job because of tides. Measuring 522ft long, it involved the sinking of hollow piles, each standing in a cast-iron disc. 'In borings, nothing but sand was found to a depth of thirty feet and in one case seventy feet', wrote engineer James Brunlees. As the viaduct prevented ships from reaching Milnthorpe, although the broad arch in the centre was designed to permit large vessels to sail through, the Railway Company, replacing an earlier wooden jetty, constructed a pier for sea-going traffic. The viaduct was improved in 1887 and, in 1914, enlarged to cope with heavier passenger trains and an increase in munitions trains. In 1915 the cast-iron viaduct was rebuilt with fifty sandstone piers.

Both Kent and Levens viaducts were constructed by Brunlees, the line over these opening in September 1857, thus completing a chain of railways around the Cumbrian coast. The Bela viaduct, carrying the line between Arnside and Hincaster Junction, had a central portion of box girder construction like the Tay and Forth bridges. Its twenty-five arches are shown in an engraving of 1896, imposing in the quiet countryside, but under Beeching's axe the structure was demolished in 1966. A violent storm destroyed ¾ mile of embankment between Arnside and Sandside on the Hincaster branch in 1884.

Walking around present day Arnside, with its grey stone Victorian and Edwardian villas, suggested this to be a good place for retirement. Many wading birds stalked the deep gullies; avocet; black-headed gulls; curlew; turnstone; cormorant; redshank. The Youth Training Centre had canoes on the estuary but there was a dearth of other sailing craft. We found a heavy, rusty anchor and chain, ghostly relics, in what was Crossfield's Beach Yard. The pier, which Arnside Parish Council bought for £100 in 1964, was rebuilt and reopened in 1984 after having been demolished by flood tides and gales.

ARNSIDE KNOTT AND TOWER

The well-wooded hill of carboniferous limestone, 521ft above sea level and overlooking the town, gives splendid viewpoints from Cartmel Fells to Tebay Falls, which can be verified by consulting Don Ainslie's engraved steel plan. We collected several pounds of blackberries to take home for jelly making and looked out for fossils of coral and shellfish showing in the rocks: ages ago Arnside Knott was an island where it is thought Vikings landed from the Isle of Man. As usual, the limestone country makes for a rich variety of flora: milkwort; thyme; tormentil; wood anemone; wild carrot; bluebell. Juniper, holly, larch, Scots pine and yew are among the trees where, legend has it, two knotted larch trees were joined together by a sailor and his bride in 1862. As this original knot on the Knott is badly decayed, Mrs Lois Marland of the National Trust mended and joined together in 1987 two new trees to take their place.

Moving on to Arnside pele tower on 9 June, where swallows and martins were swooping in and out of ruins marked with warning notices, we met a local man who, as a teenager fifty years before, had climbed to the top. Now in a dangerous condition, Arnside Tower was one of that chain of pele towers, the ring of protection, from Morecambe Bay together with that on Piel Island. 'During a mightie winde', it was burned down in 1602, but later rebuilt. In 1884 one of the huge walls blew down in another great storm when the wind 'blew a perfect hurricane for five hours and tide caused rivers to rise to a height unknown'.

In the valley and close by is Arnside Tower Farm with its large herd of black and white Friesian cows. Mr R.E. Smith worked there in the years when Robinsons farmed the land. He loved the strawberry roan shorthorn breed of those days, which gave excellent milk, rich in butterfats. But, by the 1950s, the changeover to the big black and white beasts with high milk yield had come. In Mr Smith's farm-working days, water was collected in a large water tank and some came from a spring on the Knott.

SILVERDALE

It is possible that 'the land of Soever the Northman', who arrived via Morecambe Bay, is the present Silverdale. Once, the cove had ships that called regularly but, because of silting, this village on the River Kent was left inland in the 1920s. The capricious river has changed its course on more than one occasion by such natural phenomena as the mountainous seas of 11 November 1977 that washed over the Lancashire and Cumbrian coasts, rushed up river estuaries and broke sea walls. In the 1920s the Kent reached the sea further westwards. There was sea bathing until 1860 and steamers called with holidaymakers from Morecambe.

At Jenny Brown's Point, copper from Cragfoot was smelted at a mill on the shore. The old chimney still serves as a landmark for the cross-sands route. In the 1870s Silverdale men worked at Northern Quarries Company and flax grown at Yealand was spun in the village. Several large fish were reported caught off this coast: a sturgeon weighing 156lb; 400lb of salmon taken on the same day; three porpoises on 2 July 1832, one of which weighed a ton.

A scheme in 1864 promoted by Mr H. Qualduck hoped to reclaim the sands and gain land for agriculture by building a wall from Jenny Brown's Point, between Park Point and Bolton-le-Sands. It was to stretch towards the sea for ¾ mile. Many Irishmen came to Silverdale to work on this reclamation, but the scheme was abandoned after £84,000 had been spent.

Gradually the wall became hidden by sand. The work of tidal forces and the silting continued until the wild night of 11 November 1977 when the Kent changed course and the wall was again revealed. The flood surge heaped up great piles of cockles that had to be carted away as the smell was offensive.

Mrs Gaskell, the novelist, lived at Lindeth Tower, Gibraltar Point, Silverdale, where she spent the summer of 1855. She wrote: 'Looking down on the Bay with its slow moving train of crossers led by the Guide, a small man sitting stern on his white horse better to be seen . . . The Guide may be heard blowing an old ram's horn trumpet.' Charlotte Bronte also stayed here as a girl.

We followed the small track leading to Jenny Brown's Point, supposedly named after an old lady who lived there in the eighteenth century, and then on to the National Trust area of 200 acres overlooking the salt marshes of the Kent. In July the springy, sea-washed turf was pink with sea thrift. Jack Scout Land, acquired in 1982, is a beautiful area of limestone cliff top and foreshore covering sixteen acres on the edge of the estuary. To help the National Trust, old lime workers advised on the rebuilding of a dilapidated limekiln, using layers of oak logs, old walling material from Jack Scout Land and limestone. The kiln was successfully fired and it is hoped that lime mortar may be used on National Trust farms and cottages.

On the day we explored the 106 acres of Eaves Wood, with its great variety of flora, for a short time we were completely lost, the first occasion I ever recall walking in a circle, but fortunately one special area of fissured limestone pavement which I recognised put us on the right track.

OVER SANDS

Hest Bank was where the old coaches took to the sands. A steamer, the Windermere, could, in the 1840s, come up the bay from Liverpool and anchor here, off-loading hoops and wooden articles. Hest Bank Hotel was a posting halt, its stables holding sixteen horses, six ostlers, and four drivers. Foot warmers were provided in the coaches and a good rescue service. We read that '130 people were rescued from the Sands and cared for at the Hotel'. From here it is 11 miles to Kents Bank. Hest Bank Hotel used to be the Sands Inn, where a lantern was kept in the upper room for guiding travellers and Bank House Farm, Silverdale, did likewise. Mr Hoggart's

Warning of quicksands.

public house at Silverdale saved four strangers in 1842, one ingrate going off the following morning without paying his bill.

Mail coaches ran all over the country's main roads by 1874, but the high road over the Sands of Leven, Kent and Ulverston was unique. A coach plied daily between Hest Bank and Ulverston 'as tide permitted', the old saying being that Kent and Keer had parted many a man and his mare. Between the sixteenth and nineteenth centuries more than 140 people were drowned, most of them buried at Cartmel Priory. Coaches were blown over or stuck in quicksand, horses and people drowned: two rushcutters near Silverdale; seven farmhands returning from a hiring fair; nine young people returning from Ulverston Whit Fair 'when their cart went into Black Scars Hole'; Jane Dickinson from Milnthorpe, a wife and her four children. Indeed, a refuge consisting of a ladder, platform on four wooden pillars, and a bell was suggested, 'many travellers having been lost on the sands'. Subscriptions were collected at three points including Cartmel where models could be seen, but the idea never went further.

Cedric and Olive Robinson outside Guides Farm, 1987. Cedric is the official Sands Guide and has taken the Duke of Edinburgh across.

Robert the Bruce crossed on a warlike raid. John Wesley advised: 'No stranger should go this way; there are four sands to pass.' After the railway was built few attempted the crossing, but Mr Walling, farmer from Silverdale, was 'quick-sanded' in 1876. What was true of more than a century ago holds well to this day. 'The variable nature of channels crossing the ever-shifting sands increases the danger, for the safe path today might lead to destruction tomorrow.'

Today's travellers are warned: 'Do not attempt to cross without the official guide'. Much preparatory work has to be done by the guide. Sometimes, because of strong winds and heavy rainfall, which combine to form the highest tides, parties cannot go at all. Cedric Robinson as the guide over Kent Sands and Alfred Butler, the guide over the Leven estuary, hold their offices under the Duchy of Lancaster. On 30 May 1985, in perfect conditions, under Cedric's guidance, the Duke of Edinburgh and eleven other four-in-hand carriages made another historic crossing.

Our morning with Cedric and Olive Robinson was one of the happiest encounters. Time flew as we listened to the official Sands Guide's anecdotes, for he was 'born to cockling', following the sands like his father before him, but there are now few families left who gather cockles. During hundreds of years of history, Guides Farm, with its 12-acre smallholding, black oak beams, stone staircases and blocked upper windows, was often flooded by high tides. There is a Guides Farm clock still in the area, bearing the salt tidemark. The high railway embankment has taken the view but remedied flooding. From May until September Cedric is very busy guiding parties of up to 400, for interest in the walk between Hest Bank and Kents Bank has increased enormously in the last decade.

6

West Side Story

Poetess Felicia Hemans wrote in a letter: 'Mr Wordsworth not only admired our exploit in crossing the Ulverston sands as a deed of derring-do, but as decided proof of taste'. Never could I be persuaded to emulate her, so I can cross to the western side of the Estuary only in spirit, actually to Humphrey Head where, but a few weeks earlier, Cedric Robinson, armed with railway sleepers, and a friend with a JCB, performed their deed of derring-do in rescuing a new Range Rover driven onto the beach by a visitor. Beyond the causeway, on what seemed firm sand, the vehicle had suddenly listed into an abyss. This reminded us of a Lindale anecdote. When John Wilkinson's iron coffin was transported across the sands in the nineteenth century, the hearse slumped and bearers had to run for their lives and collect the coffin later! 'Th' owld Ironmaster' was apparently a handful to the last.

Rothay, paddle steamer, 1870.

HUMPHREY HEAD

To climb the 160ft high Humphrey Head with its treacherous tides, one of Lancashire's very few cliffs, is acknowledged to be dangerous, but flagger Edward Smith and his schoolmates did so as boys, bird-nesting. Eagles once flew there, and the Holy Well Spa, St Agnes, at the foot of the cliff, with its seemingly inexhaustible supply of water, became famous medicinally. Particularly favoured by lead miners, who drank it by the gallon and washed in it, it was also a source of water, collected at low tide by the monks from Chapel Island. At a tiny cottage there lived old Rachel, a fisherman's wife who smoked a clay pipe and had a fund of stories while she sold her herbal remedies and draughts of the brackish water, which incidentally was also sold to trippers on Morecambe promenade.

Legend has it that the last wolf in England was cornered and killed in Fairy Cove on top of the Head. Sir Edgar Harrington of Wraysholme Tower promised half his lands and his niece Adela in marriage to whoever slew the wolf. It must have created havoc, as did the escaped Allendale wolf, which savaged forty sheep before it was struck by the Midland Express train near Carlisle on 29 December 1904. Wraysholme, anciently Raisholm, the only pele tower in Cartmel area, became a farm of the Morris family for centuries.

Known to old residents as South and East Plain, two farms, along with others, are said to have been washed away by encroaching tides. Alan Benson, who died in 1983, used to take passengers for a 'ramble by tractor and trailer' across the mudflats for £2. Eleven miles for a safe run, avoiding quicksands, averaged fifteen miles' travelling and Alan had to be constantly aware that tides came in at the rate of twenty-nine knots.

KENTS BANK

One description of the Kent estuary tells of 'no fewer than forty carts and chaises with men, women and dogs, all in the river at once, waves dashing through wheels, horses up to the breast in water – a scene of grotesque confusion.' This was the point where coaches arrived and travellers heaved a great sigh of relief. The abbot of Furness had a house built in 1160 known as Abbot Hall, the site now occupied by a Methodist holiday home. On our first visit the tide was ebbing with amazing swiftness, revealing tussocks of grass, old cart tracks, birdprints in mud and two distant barnacle geese, the sole occupants of a seemingly infinite expanse of beaten pewter. As the sun emerged, this great tract turned to silver then back again to grey in fleeting rain. Suddenly we got our first sighting of rubicund, yellow-oilskinned Cedric

Kents Bank House, refuge for over-sands travellers.

Robinson approaching with a very wet and sandy school party from St Bees, strung behind him like a scattered tube of Smarties.

FLOOKBURGH

Once an ancient market town, its charter of incorporation granted in 1278, Flookburgh, which is now a mile from the sea, had many inns for the travellers who had to wait up to twelve hours to cross Leven Sands. In those days the sea was close enough to wash into Flookburgh Square. Opposite the Hope and Anchor into which, we were told, is built the old village maypole, is the Market Cross. At the Crown, in 1675, Charles II was reputed to have lived on cockles. Like Milnthorpe, Flookburgh was hit by plague, brought by second-hand clothing from London, killing so many that victims could not be buried in consecrated ground. A fire in 1680 destroyed almost the entire village.

Flookburgh regalia of the historic town, photographed in the nineteenth century. Shrimping and cockling on Flookburgh's shores go back many years. Rakes, riddles, baskets, 'the jumbo' to loosen cockles, heavy carts and horses were the tools of a trade not for the inexperienced. This was proved by the deaths of twenty-one Chinese migrant workers in 2004.

Cark and Cartmel were also once coastal like Flookburgh, busy with shrimping, fishing and cockling, using purse seine nets for trawling shrimps and heavy carts with big horses, seventeen hands high, to collect cockles. As soon as the tide turned, carts flocked away from Humphrey Head, Flookburgh, Allithwaite, Cart Lane and Kents Bank, with up to twenty-eight carts working together. Les Butler, one of the few remaining Flookburgh fishermen who go to the sands at low tide, uses the Jumbo, a 4ft 6in board that agitates the sand and brings cockles to the surface where they are scooped up with the cram. In the late nineteenth century this was considered to be a 'destructive, short-sighted tool' because small cockles were crushed under its weight, so use of a 'riddle' was enforced to ensure future harvests. The fluke of flounder is caught by soke nets, which must be attended on the ebb before the gulls get to the fish. A century ago 150 men 'worked on the sands' – there was safety in numbers – but it has now dropped to very few. In the busy days a processing factory was built at Cark and special trains used to rush the sea harvest to London's famous shop, Harrods.

The Age Concern van was in the village square for 'toe nail and hair cutting' on the day we arrived and met a lively, disputatious knot of 'Flookburgh over 60s'. The 1900 church of St John the Baptist, built by Blairs of Allithwaite from Paley and Austin plans, the cost met by the Cavendish family, replaced the small chapel in the centre of the village. The ancient chapel was difficult to demolish as it had very thick stone walls. We had been told that the church housed the Charter of Flookburgh, but this was not on view and the borough's ancient regalia was available only in photograph form.

Cark Hall belonged successively to the Pickerings, Curwens and Rawlinsons. Once a busy village, Cark is the point at which the River Eaa, which rises on Newton Fell, becomes salty.

ALLITHWAITE

In the days, fifty years ago, when Mrs Burton of Burton's Farm had to take her butter all the way for sale to Allithwaite Co-op, there was rifle-range practice for soldiers in an area known as Rougham, where schoolboys searched for empty cartridge cases and rumour has it that a whole locomotive destined for Holker became 'quick-sanded'. All round are travellers' tales of the sands, how walking in such areas produces 'foot flash', a small rainbow in front of each step. In some places 'not even a nimble cat' could proceed, but boys knew, if caught up to the hips, to spread out their jacket and crawl on that.

The village swooned in a heat wave haze as we called at Pedlar's Pack, near the Royal Oak where Anne and Frank Bonnett live, thankful to escape the hurly burly of London life. A vista of golden gorse and full-bloom peonies in this 'thwaite' or clearing of Eilifr brightened our lunch break. My old copy of Mrs Beeton's cookery book, purchased in Oxford, is inscribed 'Roseheath, Allithwaite' and once belonged to J. Charnley. We sought Roseheath, but there are many buildings new among the old, dressed limestone erections and it remained out of our grasp. St Mary's church, built in 1865 on a hillside overlooking Morecambe Bay, has some wonderful views. The Bonnett's collection of old postcards from the days of the horse and cart is absorbing. Their property was once Laburnum House, in turn a vicarage, a grocer's, a painter and decorator's, a bank, now an antique shop, the age of the building being revealed in structural alterations. Mr Moorby, living next door, who has known Allithwaite all his life, recalls the bombing of the village in 1941 when incendiary bombs were dropped, probably intended for Barrow-in-Furness. He remembers that many of the houses were converted barns. Adwins, Robinsons and Thompsons were well known families who lived in Allithwaite, some working at the quarry.

CARTMEL

The ancient Priory Church of St Mary and St Michael, built between 1190 and 1440, dominates this lovely village. The position of its tower is unusual. People travel miles to see the east window of medieval glass, a 200-year-old umbrella and a first edition of Spenser's Faerie Queen. Like Allithwaite and Grange, with their open seascapes, Cartmel further inland is one of the churches of the rural Deanery of Windermere. The year 1988 saw the celebrations of the 800th anniversary, when

The Swan Hotel at Newby Bridge. Rigg's coaches called here, but the Swan had a private coach of its own and catered for cyclists when the craze hit the country in the late nineteenth century.

the priory had a new set of bells, in place by Christmas 1987. Bell tower captain Mrs Monica Wright said: 'We can't do anything with the four big ones because they are so ancient, but two bells installed in 1932 are to be re-hung with a new set of four cast in Holland.' The oak frame will be replaced with a steel structure. Since the time of the Augustinian canons, Cartmel has seen the great Scottish raids of 1316 to 1322 and the dissolution of the monasteries with its attendant damage. Thomas Holcroft, acting for Henry VIII, had the priory roof removed, but because it was also used as parish church it escaped the fate that befell most monasteries, although looting and desecration took place. The church was re-roofed in 1618 when canopies were provided for the choir stalls and misericords, the Piper Choir having the only original roof.

This peaceful village surrounded by fells was, in the eighteenth century, the most isolated in England. Walking round it, we saw the River Eea and the Cartmel Priory gatehouse, a fortified tower, used as a courthouse. This also escaped destruction in 1537 at the time of the dissolution. Between 1625 and 1790 it was used as a school and now has a small museum administered by the National Trust.

The Eea, the Winster (the old boundary between Lancashire and Westmorland), the Kent and the Keer watered the old parish. Ancient routes led over to the fells from Cartmel. Some travellers undertaking the perilous over-sands crossing would stay overnight at the priory, which in ancient times held special divine service in the oratory on Chapel Island. Children still roll dyed, hard-boiled eggs in Eastertide egging games at 'the sand bank by the rocky ground', which is the meaning of Cartmel, formerly called Churchtown. Once there was cockfighting.

'The Ferry Boat on Windermere Water.' A vintage photograph by Alfred Pettitt.

Cartmel races, c. *1920.*

Modern Cumbria boasts two racecourses, Carlisle and Cartmel, but at one time there were thirty venues, Kendal Races 'on the old course' being advertised in 1792. A field at Ladyforde, near Burneside Hall, was used in 1820. Kendal's King's Arms Hotel was one run by the racehorse breeder and father of John Singleton, a great Kendal-born rider who died in a poorhouse, aged ninety. The Kendal annual steeplechase started at Mint House, following stretches of Rivers Kent and Sprint, with fourteen watercourses and thirty-four walls to conquer. Park racecourses, like that of Cartmel, were open daily to paying customers in the 1890s.

Cartmel Races are held on Whit Saturday and Whit Monday, and over the same weekend, a hound trail is organised. Steeplechases in Cartmel Park are important events, when Dudley Moffat's Cartmel Stables of racehorses are very busy. Cartmel National Hunt race meeting takes place during the summer bank holiday.

The date of 5 August 1987 was the occasion of the 105th Cartmel Agricultural Society with prizes valuing £3,000 and seventy-seven silver challenge cups and trophies. Special attractions were: Brian Bowden's sheepdog demonstration; Flookburgh Silver Band; jumping competitions and three hound trails. It is indeed the most picturesque and comprehensive show in the north, attracting 7 to 10,000 people. A snip for senior citizens at the reduced entry rate of £1, the highlight of this traditional country show is the grand parade led by the champion heavy horse.

HOLKER HALL

Although versed in pronunciations as Hooker, we found the locals pronounced the ancestral home of the Prestons, Lowthers, Dukes of Devonshire and Cavendish family, Holker. Mid-May found these mosses brilliant with hawthorn blossom, where peat for the spartan Flookburgh cottages was cut, now an area overgrown with alder. The three villages of Cark, Flookburgh and Holker formed one township in the 1800s. Holker Hall was a house that Queen Mary loved and the Duke of Edinburgh stays every year for the week of horse trials. One feels the closeness of the River Leven joining the Kent estuary, especially at the periphery of the caravan site, on the Holker estate, at the other end of which rises Barker Scar, a typical springy-turfed limestone bluff, with its view of Chapel Island.

In summer the park and gardens are beautiful. Close by is the Leven railway viaduct which the Cavendish family had an important hand in making. Today's mansion is mainly Victorian as the 7th Duke of Devonshire commissioned Paley and Austin to design and build the west wing over a period of 3½ years, after it had been completely destroyed by fire together with many treasures. This working estate, where tree planting is a skilful feature, extends to the River Kent and the sea.

GRANGE-OVER-SANDS

The tides that once flooded Guides Farm before the making of Furness Railway also reached as far as the main street in Grange-over-Sands. A.M. Wakefield tells of the day when the little schoolhouse door burst open to let in rushing waters which careered through the back door, carrying the school clock with them, 'much to the delight of the little scholars'.

Steamy nostalgia. Furness Railway locomotive 0–6–0, Class D1, Number 18, built in 1871 but renumbered 24 in 1900. It was withdrawn in 1910.

Grange-over-Sands pier, 1900.

Once a small port, the 'grange' or granary for Cartmel Priory gave the little fishing village its name. With the railway, rapid growth ensued and promotion to 'a place of considerable resort for sea-bathing, the Torquay of the North' came. By 1853 the town had its own church and the parishioners no longer needed to trek over the Fairy Steps to Beetham. The church's first incumbent minister, the Revd Mr Rigg, experienced a baptism in the over-sands journey to take up his living, having to be carried by other passengers from the coach, which was later washed up on Holme Island.

The ornamental gardens, created by Anthony Benson, are where the beach was and had a remarkably pure spring, one of many renowned in the area. Even though washed by salt tides, shortly after the ebb the water was fresh again.

In its heyday there were two piers, a wooden erection which, neglected, later fell, and Clare House Pier from which Richard Burrow, a boatman, took Victorian parties out to Holme Island. The popularity of boating in the Kent estuary led to Crossfield's making many rowing boats. 'Buff' Butler, a former Sands Guide, took people to Holme Island on foot. Sir Christopher Philipson, having 30 acres of pleasant grounds, owned the Holme, a large mansion house. In the past the land belonged to the Barons of Kendal.

Eggerslack Woods and Hampsfell are still favourite walks from Grange-over-Sands. Revd Thomas Remington, the vicar of Cartmel, built the hospice on Hampsfell in about 1830 as a refuge for travellers, and it affords splendid views in clear weather, running to the edge of the bay. A sheltered position and good soil produces beautiful gardens in a gracious town. The largest Rose Show in the north-west, to which growers come from all over the country, is held at Grange-over-

Grange-over-Sands and Morecambe Bay, c. 1880.

Sands. A welcome sight in early spring is drifts of cowslips tumbling down garden slopes. We bought roots from the Garden Centre by the shore but alas they pined for their native heath and did not survive on our clay soil.

LINDALE

Lindale's notorious hill, which I remember cycling up soon after the Second World War broke out, caused many accidents until the village was bypassed in 1976. A black iron obelisk immediately catches the eye as you enter Lindale, commemorating the nineteenth-century ironmaster, John Wilkinson. John, born in a market cart, became a great industrialist, 'the father of iron', starting with a small furnace at Backbarrow, where he successfully produced, with his father Isaac, useful items like smoothing irons. He sailed the world's first iron boat, using the River Winster for ferrying peat to his furnace at Wilson House, Lindale. Several furnaces later, he made guns for the Napoleonic wars and cast-iron pipes for the water supply of Paris. He drained Castle Head Marsh and built his home, Castle Head, now a Field Centre, blasting holes in the rock, where he stored iron coffins in readiness for his family's afterlife, even offering one as a present to a guest. Known as a 'freethinker', he was locally unpopular because of Sunday employment. His monument was struck by lightning and his coffin 'quicksanded'; it was thought by some old residents that the Castle Head area was haunted. Undoubtedly a remarkable man who collaborated with James Watt when the father of iron met the father of steam!

MEATHOP MOSSES

A bronze celt was found at Meathop, which was then a turf-cutting area, in 1850 when the British Archaeological Association were busy touring the Kent area. On the estuary side of the A590 road, Meathop Moss is now a nature reserve rich in wildlife, home of the magpie and shelduck, who frequent coastal marshes beside the sandy, muddy estuary, and of lapwing whose eggs were collected in thousands last century to be eaten, but which, under the 1981 Wildlife and Countryside Act, are now protected. Ulpha (the place of the Wolf), Meathop and Witherslack once came within the bounds of the large parish of Beetham. 'Brogden's sea wall' (the engineer involved with Brunlees in the building of the Leven Viaduct), gave way under tremendous tidal pressure. Haystacks were carried a mile and many sheep died. A golf course, drainage ditches and spinneys of silver birch are now features of a wide area, part of which recently has been threatened with rubbish dumping.

From the car I saw descriptive names fitting well the area: Mill Side; Beck Head; Moss House; Sampool and finger posts directing to Ulpha and Witherslack. With time running out one August evening we chose the latter. John Barwick, a native of this area, was also a benefactor of this village separated into three parts by small hills and situated past Yewbarrow. He became Dean of St Paul's, London, but did not forget the place of his birth in his 1671 will, a clause of which enabled the village to buy land for a graveyard. Before that the villagers had to make the perilous trip across the sands, bearing the body in the parish coffin. The church at Witherslack also came about through his generosity.

Today's Derby Arms has on show the head of an enormous stag shot on Whitbarrow Scar in 1912, but one old-timer remembered that the Bear Café had gone one better with a stuffed bear, which from his description I can only think must have been from the days when dancing bears were taken round the country. My mother remembered an occasion in 1892 when as a young child she had backed into a bear with its trainer and was terrified. 'Swills' were once made here as a cottage industry: baskets for animal food were made from oak spills cut from coppice woods at Bigland and Backbarrow, the method being 'cut down, boil and lap round with a hazel bough'.

Witherslack was one of our last calls of that year. Swallows and house martins were gathering on the wires in ever-increasing numbers, the young swallows distinguishable by their shorter tail-streamers and paler undersides. Autumn was truly upon us and we turned for home with the slightly sad, still feeling that the end of summer always brings.

This travelling performing bear, seen here with Mr Perman in about 1875 was 'trained by kindness'. A female bear, she was said to be very fond of him. On their travels together they slept in barns. The Witherslack bear was probably also a performing bear.

7

A Mysterious Monument

Motorcars to Eddie were serious business. After all he was the driver. In my more frivolous days I christened one of our cars K-K-K-Katy because of its number plate and my pseudonym Kate Houghton, but there was another reason. Frequently we would drive to Kentmere, Kendal and on to Keswick especially when we had the caravan and holidays came round. These were good opportunities to call in on Annie, shepherdess of the fells and known for miles around. Once we walked over Red Pike to reach her cottage. On another occasion we approached from Haystacks and Green Gable. Real 'fell folks' go over the top. It is a long way round by road.

When the summer rush of traffic was at its height on the A591 it was a treat to stop at Staveley once again, to leave the lemmings to it and further explore this

Eddie with 'Piebald', in our secret valley, Beckside Farm, Marthwaite.

A ruined watermill on the River Kent, Sawmill Cottage, Kentmere.
(Courtesy of Kendal Library)

backwater at the foot of Kentmere Valley lying midway between Windermere and Kendal on the river Kent.

Situated in an old wood mill we found Wilf's Café. Remnants of the old mill can be seen. There were once eight (some people said six) water-powered mills at Staveley serving fullers, smelters, flour millers, and spinning spindle and bobbin makers. At nearby Ings is a Watermill Inn. The River Kent flows through Staveley and behind Wilf's Café runs the River Gowan. Here at Staveley the two rivers join. Peter Hall, the woodcarver, explained to us that water power from the Gowan river was used in Staveley from 1135 until 1971 when the last powered mill closed.

Leaving Staveley and travelling towards Kendal we searched for the Elba monument, an obelisk originally without any inscription. Kendal library had the answer. The monument was put up by James Bateman of Tolson Hall who much admired William Pitt and his part in the defeat of Napoleon Bonaparte – 'the pilot who weathered the storm', was Mr Bateman's enthusiasm for the statesman but when Napoleon escaped from the island of Elba the glowing inscription was omitted. But not for ever.

Left: *The Elba Monument off the A591 north of Kendal was erected in 1814 by James Bateman of Tolson Hall. James Cropper's paper company celebrated its 100th anniversary in 1989. Charles Cropper, descendant and new owner of Tolson Hall, placed the plaque on the monument in 1914: 'William Pitt, the pilot that weathered the storm'.*

Below: *A class of schoolchildren (or it may have been the whole school) with the headmaster, at Staveley, c. 1890.*

The lagoon-shaped Kentmere tarn can be seen following the road from Staveley towards Maggs Howe. The first tarn drained in 1840 was intended to give place to much needed grazing land but that was when diatomite, mentioned earlier, was discovered. From 1930 to 1971 mining went on. Once it ceased the long, narrow stretch was flooded to form the new Kentmere Tarn.

On a day of fitful sunshine with shadows racing across the fells we tackled Nan Bield Pass, which brought us to Mardale.

Ings, near Staveley, was where the wealthy merchant, James Bateman of monument fame was born. He made a generous contribution to the building of St Anne's church in 1743 but sadly he never saw its completion in the town of his birth. He died returning from Italy along one of his trade routes and the poet William Wordsworth remembered him in the poem Michael: the poor boy 'made good' has his story told in these lines:

> There's James Bateman, thought she to herself,
> He was a parish boy – at the church door
> They made a gathering For him, shillings, pence,
> And half pennies, Wherewith the neighbours bought
> A basket, Which they filled with pedlar's wares.
> And, with this basket on his arm, the lad
> Went up to London, found a master there
> Who, out of many, chose the trusty boy
> To go and overlook his merchandise
> Beyond the seas; where he grew wondrous rich,
> And left estates and monies to the poor.
> And at his birthplace built a chapel floored
> With marble . . .

Heversham, only a mile away from Levens Hall and close to the estuary of the River Kent was also worthy of more than one visit because of its still tangible links with antiquity. A charming village, we found villagers especially proud of one particular treasure, which can be traced back to King Alfred's day. It is a stone in the church porch, severely worn, but a part of a cross carved with grapevines and a vixen with cubs.

Heversham Hall, dating from the sixteenth century, has a massively walled courtyard and a fragment of a tower, possibly built two centuries earlier. More things to be proud of are the school, built when Shakespeare was writing his plays, and a seventeenth-century sundial in the churchyard. Also traced back to the seventeenth century are the altar rails and heraldic glass. Ephraim Chambers' Dictionary of Art and Science, already mentioned, was praised by none other than Dr Samuel Johnson, who admitted his own style of writing owed much to this brilliant scholar, one of many educated in the limestone school so long ago.

SNUFFING IT

Any regular watcher of The Antiques Roadshow will have noticed how frequently snuff boxes are mulled over. Mull is the most apt word for that was the word associated with the box when the partaking of snuff (the brown powder made from pounded tobacco) came into fashion from the sixteenth century onwards. Craftsmen produced many charming versions of this little box – enamel, filigree, precious metal. The wealthier you were, the more decorative your mull and with what pride a Georgian dandy may have asked another young buck: 'Would it please you to take a snesh of my mull?' Yes, the habit of sniffing the brown powder through the nose, a pinch at a time, was called 'sneshing'.

When tobacco arrived in England from the New World during Queen Elizabeth I's reign, taking snuff became more popular than actually smoking the tobacco through a pipe. We all know how the story goes that a wench carrying a bucket of water drenched Sir Walter Raleigh as he took his first puff. The lass thought her master was on fire. No such hazards with snuff-taking. One could partake on the sly or a sleight of hand in a flurry of lace cuffs. All more appealing to the ladies of whom perhaps some quickly caught the habit.

How snuff was discovered sounds off another story that seems quite likely. The tobacco was transported from place to place by pack mules over very rough tracks and terrain. Rather like the dust from tea, destined for tea bags, at the end of a long, jolting journey heaps of snuff were found readily prepared in the packs of 'wantahs', strapped to the mules' backs. It saved pounding up with pestle and mortar, which was the original sixteenth-century method.

It was claimed that this powder gave protection against the many pestilences and plagues that were present down the ages – another important reason for the spread of its popularity. Some people still believe this is a fact.

In 1702, Admiral Rooke captured hundreds of barrels of snuff from a Spanish galleon and it was said he paid his crew with his haul – a change from paying them with rum perhaps. There is no doubt at all that the habit spread throughout all social classes and by the 1730s a factory was opened devoted to producing and marketing 'the brown stuff'.

Kendal became an important town for many reasons but one of them was 'snuffing it'. The Puritans regarded the habit as so wicked and injurious that the term came down as synonymous with courting death but that did not stop the taking of it. From prince to pauper all indulged. In Turkey its use did indeed invoke the death penalty.

Although rained off on our first attempt to reach Helsington we determined to find out more and hopefully get photographs, for the snuff of dreams apparently came to Kendal via Scotland. By packhorse? Snuff-making machinery also found its way to Kendal and the obvious answer was to use a waterpower mill on the River Kent. A Mr Harrison produced his famous 'Kendal Brown' as early as 1790. In the Fylde of Lancashire, James Baines, a prosperous woollen draper, offered tobacco and snuff as a sideline to his main source of wealth. An 'instrument for spinning tobacco' was listed in the inventory following his death.

*A packhorse bridge, possibly Rossill Bridge, Bannisdale, in another beautiful study by
Alfred Pettitt, c. 1860. The smallest of the bridges over the River Mint, it was replaced
by a larger bridge without the beauty. Established as early as 1860, Pettitt was a
skilled artist. With his gifted daughter Lucie he ran an art gallery. Two years
before his death Manchester Corporation purchased a set of his pictures for
the State Room of the recently built Manchester Town Hall.*

He was snuffing it even earlier than Mr Harrison (James Baines died in 1717).
But Thomas Harrison's, now the oldest snuff working machinery in the country,
still exists in Kendal.

Through marriage, the business came down to Samuel Gawith who later was to
become one of the mayors of Kendal. Further additions brought about the firm
of Gawith, Hoggarth and Company in 1887 that operated from Helsington Mill
premises, which were once used for fine cut freestone. Snuff became as popular as
'Woodbine Willies', the poor man's cigarette, but the true aficionado, not living
in the underworld of Charles Dickens's Mrs Gamp, well knew and still knows one
grade of snuff from another.

We even heard of a Snuff Mill Meadow that we traced to a mill powered by a beck
from the River Kent in Natland, near Kendal. The directories of the old grey town
are rich in snuffy references.

WOOL IS MY BREAD – SET TO MUSIC

The lovely market town of Kendal has a puzzling motto: Pannus Mihi Panis – which epitomises an idea traceable to 1331 when Edward III granted Kendal a Weavers' Charter, making it the chief centre of wool-weaving in the north of England. English archers wore the tough cloth, known as Kendal Green, and for 600 years that industry thrived. So – back to the motto, wool was the town's bread.

Richard Coeur-de-Lion had made Kendal a barony in 1189, the Romans had established bases near the town and the Saxons had occupied it. On the south aisle of the parish church can be seen a shaft from a stone cross dating AD 850. But over the years Scottish borderers tormented the 'auld grey town'. Dr Manning's Yard is an example of past refuge for Kendal inhabitants; the steep, narrow alleys known as yards or courts were designed to keep out invaders. Many of the Flemish weavers settled in these enclaves. Perhaps they also needed protection.

The Old Market Cross or Call Stone near the town hall was where the monarchs of England were proclaimed. Do not miss the thirteenth-century parish church of Holy Trinity with its five aisles. It is one of the largest in England. Sir Walter Scott, in his novel Rokeby, describes the stormy entrance into this church by Robin Philipson, a Royalist supporter, hell-bent on revenge over the Roundhead, Colonel Briggs.

Tudor domestic architecture, well-preserved, is to be seen in the castle dairy, which was built in 1564, the year Shakespeare was born.

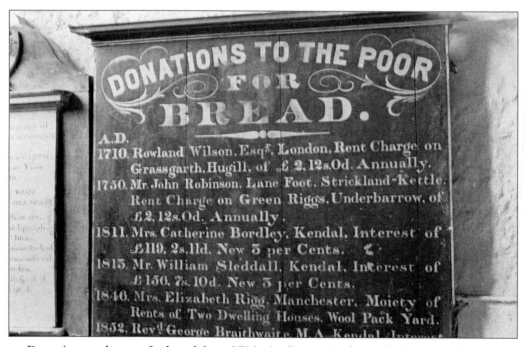

Donations to the poor for bread from 1710. An 'interesting' record of rents and interest from property that benefited the poor from landowners in Kentmere.

Bullocks and calves in melting snow, Kentmere, February 1971.

We were lucky enough to hear a carillon played from the high town hall tower, English, Welsh, Scottish and Irish tunes. It sounded lovely with high blue skies, white clouds, and bracing air supplied with delicious, meaty scents from the pie shop.

After the long day sightseeing and trekking up and around this hilly town we thankfully worked our way back to The Grove, Kentmere 'old farm house' in delightful surroundings, tea and accommodation, the telephone number for which was once Kentmere 48.

It was a wet August in the main and the Kendal Caving Club had been exploring 'Lost John's System'. Some of them were also glad to lay down their heads that night.

The black marble font, dating from the fifteenth century, was the last thing I remembered before dropping off to sleep.

KENDAL GALA

The rugby field at Kendal, we were told, around 5 August, annually attracted Cumberland and Westmorland wrestlers flexing muscles and hounds straining at their leashes, the latter ready to set off on a 10-mile circuit of the fells. Almost every villager from far around came to this event which had been held since 1869 and was organised by Friendly Societies eager to help widows and orphans. Prize money in 1888, the year my mother was born, totalled ninety guineas. In August 1899 it took place in Maudes Meadow and Bank Fields, the old rugby centre. Bank Fields, later known as Noble's Rest, was a grandstand provided by nature itself for champion viewing. Revived in 1949 the Gala raised £1,700 for the mayor of Kendal's Homes for the Aged appeal fund.

A great supporter of the gala was Joe Millward who had attended annually since 1890. T.L. Hall was treasurer when the Walker brothers were champions in the penny-farthing cycle races. Professor Kent made an ascent by balloon followed by a parachute descent. Morris dancers, 'the original cycling coon', the great athletes the 'Lodge brothers' and others drew crowds and 'a thrilling and lightning flight, 200 to 400ft through the air' ushered in the age of the aeroplane.

Admission to the gala was a mere sixpence. You could buy beef and ham sandwiches for fourpence (old money remember), meat pies for tuppence and stone ginger beer bottles for tuppence. Alas these old-style galas finished in 1902 but the stories are still told. Jack Alderson had a goose that followed him everywhere. 'He was invited to come along to the Gala Field with his goose and a race was planned in which Jack had a start of twenty yards, the sprint being 120.' The goose reached the tape first!

8

'Memories are Made of This'

Some wise person said 'man needs memory as a tree needs roots' and fortunately our combined long-term memories were very good. It was Eddie (a lover of Uncle Joe's Mint Balls) who remembered the Original Daffy's Elixir, beloved by his great-grandfather for its warming qualities. I found out that Mr Ashburner, bookseller and stationer in Kendal, 'and no other person in the town' was sent consignments from London to sell by the River Kent 'this original elixir which exceeded all medicines ever prepared . . . the only family medicine ever prepared. . . . Daffy's appeared to be family friendly for it promised to cure everything, even dropsy and consumption – 'cured . . . amongst many hundreds performed by this noble elixir'. Sold in the late eighteenth century, that its fame extended into the late nineteenth century was remarkable. Between March and December 1764 Thomas Pearson bought twelve bottles at 1s 3d each: it is recorded in the shop's ledgers; and also that Mr Ashburner sold many other items: stationery, groceries, cloth garments and, surprisingly, gunpowder. It is written in the account book that Mrs Brecan bought 2lb of it and 6lb of shot for 3s 5½d.

Most of the gunpowder was for use in quarries or mines; Matthew Bell, Samuel Peacock, Robert Wharton and Company at Awgill bought pounds of the stuff at 1s 1d a pound weight. Gunpowder was not produced locally until the first mills were built by John Wakefield at Sedgwick, the gunpowder being transported by coasters from Milnthorpe. At that time, there were fewer specialised shops. What is amazing are the curious items requested and supplied: '2 cruets, 3 Delft punchbowls, a pair of spurs (6s) fiddle strings (2s 3d), lime, bricks, a cart and wheels.' They also supplied lots of hand-knitted stockings, as did Abraham Dent from Kirkby Lonsdale not far away. The Dents seem to have become friends with the shopkeeper for they received welcome gifts of cockles from the Kent estuary and Morecambe Bay from time to time. No doubt that delicious memory stayed with them all down the years.

Memories of the rush carts persist because the bringing of fresh rushes to strew in churches was made into a jolly occasion everywhere, like at harvest festival time. Fresh rushes were cut at Silverdale and laid in spring when the earth was awakening after a hard winter. It was something to shout about and the decorated cart was trundled in procession. The engraving shows small boys aloft upon it, every window in the square crammed with onlookers and even two foolhardy enthusiasts on a rooftop. Barking dogs and banners completed the scene. Ambleside's rush bearing is still observed.

The rush cart, 1821.

A description of a church service at Cartmel Priory a century ago steps back into history: 'It was icy cold. Even sturdy farmers brought overcoats. There was a small brazier and a small barrel organ, that groaned, left out notes and stopped altogether. Then the wooden-clogged choir clumped down to a pew. The most curious was Bigland Pew. It was on large castors and could be moved about. It was entered by steps like an omnibus and was roofed'. The Bigland family could snore away undisturbed at sermon time! This account by A.M. Wakefield also recalls punishment stocks at the church gate, in good repair but never used in her time. All appeal to the memory and imagination.

Harvest home suppers, after the gathering-in of crops, must have been memorable. Everybody had helped, young and old and a good harvest meant lavish provision, and lots of liquid, from grateful farmers. All rejoiced. A good harvest resulted in perhaps the most important social event of the year. When the reapers had cut the last sheaf of corn it was customary to raise it in the air and give the harvest shout:

> Well ploughed, well sowed,
> Well harrowed, well mowed
> And all carted to the barn
> With never a load throwed.
> Hurrah!

Harvesting in Cumbria in the shadow of Fleetwith Pike.

Ploughing in Kentmere.

Herdwick sheep in Kentmere, c. 1930. Will they become a memory?

A rare breed of sheep in Kentmere. They came from St Kilda when the islanders left in the 1920s, leaving a deserted island for hedgehogs to colonise.

TAILOR-MADE

When a 'Sunday-best suit' was required by Kentmere farmers the tailor was asked to stay at the farm and was given board and lodging. Horse and trap collected the heavy sewing machines and 'goose' irons. This travelling from farm to farm to convert cloth into garments was known as 'whipping the cat'. Mr Holt, a tailor, stayed at Joe Bennett's Thornthwaite Farm for a week. 'It took me from Monday morning to Saturday afternoon to get through'. Mr Holt had an uncle interested in Herdwick sheep. Uncle and nephew took four days off each year to help with the sheep shearing. Some farmers boasted that the cloth was made from wool produced on their own farms.

A man's suit could cost about 2 guineas. Trousers were brought in for 'new fronts and seats'. If repair was totally impossible the garment was destined to play its part in a peg rug. Sleeved waistcoats were popular to keep out the cold and there were no turn-ups for trousers but women's long skirts were sewn with a strong braid round the bottom to prevent wear as the garment brushed the ground.

FROST AT MIDNIGHT

In February 1895 Lake Windermere froze from end to end for six weeks and the extraordinary sight of skating parties, both day and night, coaches crossing, ice yachts skimming, roast chestnut stalls and oven fires blazing on the ice, made it a never-to-be-forgotten spectacle. One schoolboy wrote: 'we spent the whole day on the ice, only leaving the steely lake at dusk when fires were burning, torches lit and our elders carried lanterns as they shot about like fireflies.' William Wordsworth's evocative description in The Prelude, of skating on frozen Windermere, shows that, over a century ago, hard winters made the event not uncommon but the 1895 'great freeze' was outstanding. Thousands of people came to see it, travelling in special trains.

A PIECE OF CAKE

The world-famous Kendal Mint Cake Shop in Westmorland Shopping Centre, Kendal, is a shop devoted to the four makers of Kendal Mint Cake: Wilson, Quiggin, Romney and Wiper. Polar explorers, climbers striving for the summit of Everest, sailors battling against 15ft waves would not set forth without it.

It must be the world's most travelled sweet, if not the most famous, as many Cumbrians claim. It was born in the mid-nineteenth century, at 78 Stricklandgate, the shop then being a favourite toffee shop, as it had been for the past forty years, and run by the Thompson family.

Joseph Wiper was there, busily producing Bulls Eyes, Barley Sugar, Butter Toffee etc. when one batch of sugar, glucose and oil of peppermint transmuted itself into Mint Cake. It is my guess that a boiling was left cooling for too long. Others say there was a definite recipe, coming from an old lady who lived a few doors away. Be that as it may, Joseph's Mint Cake was an instant best-seller. The business passed to

Robert Wiper who foresaw the success it could be, if taken on the big expeditions going on at that time. Carried on two mules and packed in airtight cases Kendal Mint Cake travelled from Darjeeling to the base camp at Everest. Kendalian and mountaineer Dr Howard T. Somervell made a point of leaving some for the Dalai Llama of Tibet. Francis S. Smythe, a hero of my rock-climbing brother, Edward, ate mint cake when he managed to reach 28,200ft. No doubt Mallory and Irvine, who perished in their attempt to reach the top of Everest, also had a supply with them. There were countless expeditions between the 1930s and 1950s, even one to track down the Abominable Snowman in 1954. One wonders how the cake might have swayed an encounter.

Little has changed in the production of this famous sweetmeat over the years and later I would be assisting Radio 4 in a series of programmes – *A Piece of Cake* – which included the famous minty slab along with Eccles Cakes, Chorley Cakes and Pontefract Cakes.

Talking of a piece of cake, the Kentmere Rum Cake came near to the perfection of my late mother's Dundee Cake. I was given the recipe after sampling at Staveley.

Kentmere Rum Cake

A rich family cake made special by soaking the fruit in rum for two days.
Place in a large bowl:
8oz raisins
8oz currants
3oz glacé cherries

Pour over these about 12 floz of rum and leave to soak.
8oz butter
12oz plain flour
1 tsp baking powder
4 eggs
8oz sugar – preferably brown
½tsp mixed spice
½tsp cinnamon

Sift the flour into a large baking bowl with the baking powder and spices. Cream butter and sugar in another bowl. Beat in the eggs one at a time and fold in half of the flour mixture. Then stir in all the fruit and fold in the remaining flour mix, gently beating, making sure all is mixed well. Grease an 8in cake tin and smooth in the cake mixture. Bake at 300° for 2½ hours. Allow to cool.

Annie Nelson (see page 140) also gave me her excellent recipe for Cumbrian Scones.

Annie Nelson's Cumbrian Scones

1lb flour
6oz lard and margarine mixed together
2tsp baking powder
3oz sultanas (stoned)
1 free-range egg
3oz sugar
Sufficient buttermilk or milk to mix

Mix together flour and baking powder. Rub in the lard and margarine. Then add sultanas and sugar with the egg and buttermilk and mix into a soft dough (leaving a little of the whisked up egg to brush over the scones). Shape into small scones or use a round cutter. Place on a baking sheet, well greased, and bake in a very hot oven for 10 minutes. The egg brushed over the scones before placing in oven gives a shiny, brown appearance.

THEY'RE OFF! RACING AT KENDAL AND CARTMEL

The origins of Kendal racing seem hazy, but handbills from 29 and 30 August 1792 refer to the 'old course near Kendal'. Early meetings were held on high land on the west side of Helsfell Nab. From all accounts a three-day meeting held in a field at Ladyford, near Burnside Hall, in September 1820 was a great success and it was resolved to form a committee to arrange annual meetings each August: 'From the time of the year on which they are fixed, there is little doubt of a full attendance.'

A new racecourse was laid on Fisher's Plain, Bradleyfield, and a similar three-day event on 7, 8 and 9 August of the following year attracted 6,000 spectators. A total of seven races were run and the 'Correct List' firmly stated: 'All dogs found on the racecourse will be destroyed.' The Westmorland Gazette reported: 'Many who were enemies to the races last year are now the most forward in promoting them. . . . Such is the extent and beauty of the prospect from that part of the ground where the start and booths are erected, it is impossible to conceive a finer promenade. In order to finance a handsome racing fund Mr Howard of the Kendal Theatre presented all its Monday receipts.' Even the national Sporting Magazine had words of praise for the new course.

The excitement of the turf attracted such owners as the Duke of Leeds to the early meetings. Horses were even brought from Newmarket to Kendal – a time-consuming business in those days. Lord Lowther was one of the stewards at the 'new races' with their continued competition for the Gold Cup. The Yeomanry Silver Cup and a Town Purse worth £50 were now also competed for. However, in spite of its good start on Fisher's Plain, 26 August 1839 witnessed a sale by public auction of the grandstand and effects.

Race suppers, known as 'ordinaries', were held at the King's Arms on Tuesdays and Thursdays and at the Commercial Inn on Thursdays after the racing. The gentry, however, revelled in a Race Ball at the King's Arms on the Wednesday evening, when ladies' fashions were stunning and smart carriages countless. The King's Arms was the obvious venue as it was once run by the racehorse breeder and father of John Singleton, jockey of the fabled horse Eclipse, winner of many races. This great, Kendal-born rider died at the age of ninety in the Chester Poorhouse, apparently quite unnoticed, in the very year that Kendal's New Course opened.

In March 1845 we hear of the Kendal Annual Steeplechase on a course of 3¾ miles, seemingly more arduous than today's Grand National. Starting near Mint House, just off the A6 north of Kendal, the course followed stretches of the Rivers Sprint and Kent 'across ploughed field rendered very heavy by the rains . . . over thirty-four fence walls and 140 water courses'. One feels very sorry for the horses, especially those that had already made a journey from the south of England.

Squire Abington or George Baird, a colourful devotee of racing, visited Kendal in the 1870s. Nationally renowned, he was only thirty-two when he died, by which time his great wealth had been squandered on horse racing and prizefighting. Professional jockeys carried his colours to victory at Epsom and Ascot, but it was

The King's Arms, Kendale, 1870s. Balls were held here at the time of the races, with the ladies in stunning gowns. Mr Ashburner's premises were near the River Kent.

Looking for the Sticky Toffee Pudding shop – but it was in Cartmel: this is a weind near Sandside.

said that his greatest pleasure was in riding his own horse, Duniguioott, at one of the provincial courses like Kendal, where in 1881 he won the Lowther and Edenhall Plate.

By the 1870s the number of racecourses began to decline, for in 1873 the Jockey Club ruled that no race should be run for less than £50, a sum raised three years later to £100. 'Park racecourses' began to appear, open only to paying customers, so the character of rural British racing on such courses as Kendal's faded away. Kendal's final meeting ended in a blaze of glory in 1882 when Charlie Cunningham won three races on Lindisfarne on the same day. As both owner and rider, 'C.J.' had been a keen supporter of Kendal Races.

Cumbria now boasts only two racecourses, Carlisle and Cartmel, but at one time there were almost thirty, including Workington, Whitehaven, Kirkby Lonsdale, Cockermouth, Keswick and minor rural meetings where racing took place once a year or even less. Cartmel is the smallest, but surely the most picturesque racecourse in Lancashire. Its spring bank holiday meeting draws huge crowds and is a real family occasion with roundabouts, sideshows, swings and candy floss. Indeed you might never see a horse as there is a fairground in the middle of the course and general visibility, even from the 'grandstand', is severely limited when the horses disappear behind the trees. But everyone is in a good mood and the bookmakers are willing to take bets ranging from just 15p.

9

Arnside, Milnthorpe and Other Lost Ports

Ten years ago a friend of ours pioneered wreck-trekking, which involves pin-pointing the many unlucky ships which came to grief in shoals and on sandbanks along the north-west coast. Not a sport for the unwary, it involves danger unless armed with tide tables, compass, flask of coffee and a good sense of direction. Twice, our friend and his wife met completely disorientated people walking towards disaster when mist had suddenly blotted out land and sky. Whenever I pass the remains of the nineteenth-century wreck Abana, almost invariably someone is pacing around its ribs with a metal detector. Wreck-trekking

A distant view, Arnside Knott.

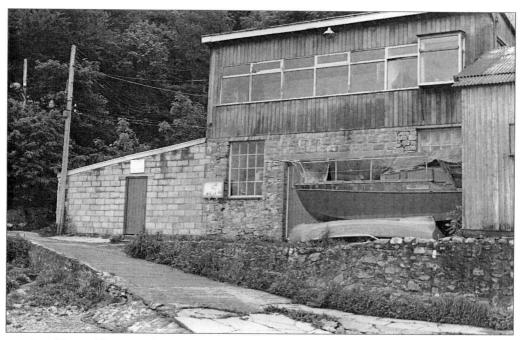

Arnside, a village on the River Kent, was where the Crossfield family built the famous Morecambe Bay prawners. It is a port with its own custom house and warehouse (now used by Arnside Sailing Club). Iron ore, charcoal and coal used to be brought here by sea, but after Brunlees railway viaduct was built in 1837, only the smallest vessels could reach the quay.

has caught on, participants now using tractors instead of foot-slogging over miles of sand flats. Nostalgia for those magnificently built schooners, scows, barques, barquentines and brigantines that once criss-crossed the sea lanes is as compelling as that for equally magnificently built iron locomotives which steamed down the railroads of the world.

Too old for wreck-trekking, we tried port-trekking, in search of small landing places, most of which now exist only in name. These were once the havens for sailing ships, although not all made happy landfall.

'Not a trace remains', say the books, but we found that, rather like old soldiers, ports tended to fade away rather than die. If indeed they died, they died hard, for it was not the 'writing on the wall', expressed in ghost-faint letters on warm brick, telling of past ships' chandlers, net braiders, dry salters, curers, but the many dark green glass floats suspended on faded rope, the ubiquitous sand, sea and anchorage references in house names, the sparkling grey, granite cobbles, pink pebbles and porridge stones, lignum dead-eyes, gnarled moss stocks and other types of jetsam ranging from helmet shells to mighty anchors, as though long-dead sailors had left instructions to preserve these relics so that the ports themselves and the role they played would never be forgotten. Reminders cropped up in gardens so close to the sea that, like the 'beach boys' of old, they were regularly dappled with spindrift and

Prima Donna, FD91, is a fishing smack built by Crossfield at Arnside in about 1900.

Francis Crossfield was registered as a boatbuilder in 1849, but by 1940 the yard had been cleared. He had a reputation for building high quality yachts and prawners. All materials were carefully selected. Fred and William were the last owners of the boatyard. We found only rusty chains and anchors on our visit. This old anchor is from a sailing ship.

sprayed with spume – a steady, pickling process. At what seemed, on a grey day, comparable to the world's end, we came upon a faded blue and gold mermaid ship's figurehead. We found in a field hard by the sea a 'coyt' roofed with an old clinker-built boat. What could be more expressive!

However, it was the stories of old inhabitants that best kept the torches burning. We heard how gangs of beach boys scrubbed and salted fish on rock platforms, each day spreading out the dry fish in the sun, each night re-stacking it into towers until entirely cured and ready for shipment. Many a beach boy, smitten with sea-fever, forsook his stacking and ran away to sea, climbing aboard one of the white-winged ships.

Sitting quietly, as we often did on our quest, munching beef sandwiches and drinking hot coffee, it was easy to conjure up scenes at these little Cumbrian ports; 'Gems,' one ex-sailor insisted, 'scenes of orderly chaos.' This was amid the varied timbre of voices, some foreign tongues, the clacking of capstan pawls as topsails went aloft, the softer scurring sound of foresail rings soaring up forestays, the grinding and groaning of a bucket dredger mingling with steam whistles, the screeching of gulls careering overhead, the bumping of last-minute, frenzied loading of stores for what could be a long sea voyage. Nearby, the shipyard would be permeated with the scents of rosin, pitch, tar, paint, new rope, sawdust and fresh-sawn pine. Shouts surely echoed from the sail-loft. Men whose minds were the blueprints for the marvellous craft they built, wielded long-handled axes and adzes in those days. When building waned at one port they were known to walk 50 miles to the next, carrying their tools, perhaps to Barrow, Liverpool or Whitehaven.

In the days of these little ports there was much cheap labour, a plentiful supply of iron for anchors, chains, fastenings, wood for masts, linen for sails. Listed under dimensions and scantlings for John Brockbank's Richard are beams, stanchions, keel, planks, elm, fir, English oak, copper, brass and 'a Europa figurehead of proper dimensions for a ship of her tonnage'. Some northern ports built for others, even for London, as here, a century ago, ship-building was cheaper.

Ye Olde Fighting Cocks Inn, Arnside.
In the nineteenth century a customs officer,
the mariner known as Captain Bush, was
landlord here when Arnside was a port.

Milnthorpe cattle fair, c. 1893. Milnthorpe used to be the only port in Westmorland which sent ships to Liverpool with salt.

Port-trekking raised many side-tracking ideas which could have taken us right off the subject into equally enticing regions of study: such compelling thoughts for example as the exporting of Kendal Green cloth from Milnthorpe. Soldiers' garments made from this are mentioned by none other than William Shakespeare. At Milnthorpe, at a bend in the River Bela, only a heavy iron ring remains in the remnant of wharf below Dallam Tower. At high water, goods were lowered into carts. Vessels settled onto the gravelly beds only to re-float with the next tide. Between 1740 and 1850, described as 'Millthrop's heyday', raw materials were unloaded at the Strands, destined for water mills up river.

Silting led to moorings being made at Sandside and Arnside. As at Arnside, the Grange shore was 'covered one hour with ships, another with pedestrians'. 'Only at certain hours is the jetty accessible to steamboats', it was reported in the Pictorial England and Wales round-the-coast survey published by Cassell in 1902. Because of the Kent river bore, carters had to work fast. Tons of sea coal were unloaded here. Nowadays only ghosts seem to haunt the Arnside shipyard of Francis John Crossfield who made this port so highly esteemed by his boat building. Into the Crossfields' 30ft Morecambe Bay prawners and yachts went local wood and workmanship akin to that of Armours and Singletons of Fleetwood. In August 1987 we found part of a large, rusting anchor and massive iron cable, overgrown with nettles, speaking eloquently of past glory. Directories reveal the importance of its trade; the sloop Leighton was built especially to carry

Market Street, Ulverston, 1920. In the far right-hand corner is the Market House. The famous engineer Sir John Rennie built a canal from Ulverston to the sea, but silting became a problem, so Barrow became the major port in the area.

iron and slate. Marble and gunpowder were handled and coal imported from Whitehaven to supplement high-grade peat cut from Meathop Mosses.

Piel, now a quiet yachting centre, used to dispatch shipments of grain and wine stored in Piel Castle by the Abbot of Furness. When Lambert Simnel landed in 1487, with 2,000 German mercenaries, that harbour was full of ships. It was the only customs port between Poulton-le-Sands and Whitehaven.

Conishead port also harked back to monastic times when Gamel de Pennington, who owned land in Ulverston and Bardsea, founded the priory (that same summer we found only a wayside sign, miles from anywhere, announcing 'Cockles and Fish For Sale'). Ulverston is now better known for its hiring fair, but William White, the last of its shipbuilders, along with his brother John, was renowned for the expert workmanship that went into twelve wooden ships. 'Every inn was full to overflowing', reported the Kendal Mercury on 24 August 1844. Many were 'Lakers' as the tourists were known, on their way to Windermere, but Ulverston was also busy as a port.

'Beware of Quicksands' is the notice overshadowing Greenodd's pleasant picnic area. Following the estuary, a long, telltale track, now grassed over, reveals where the railway line ran. Of this once-flourishing iron ore port, only rotting staithes remain. Both Greenodd and Penny Bridge were shipbuilding communities, the latter is a small landing place where a ship of 300 tons was built, but which suffered the

Greenodd was once a flourishing iron ore port and shipbuilding community when Furness ports exported 75,000 tons of the material annually. Miners were paid 1s a day. Greenodd, like Ulverston, was a creek under the port of Lancaster.

fate common to most. Silting eventually rendered it useless. For the making of gunpowder at Low Wood factory, sulphur and nitrates were brought. Coastwise from Coniston came copper and slate and 'black diamonds' from Whitehaven. But the heart-rending black cargoes were the terrified, wailing slaves left at Penny Bridge.

As for Ravenglass, like Maryport, it was thriving when Liverpool was unknown. Sea traffic supplied a large Roman coastal fort where the three rivers, Eea, Mite and Irk emptied into the estuary, affording good anchorage. Heavy silting made it difficult to find any traces of the harbour at the port in Carlisle.

In visiting such one-time ports you need to develop x-ray eyes in order to sweep aside the clutter and detritus of centuries. Perhaps the best part of port-trekking was resting in some quiet pub after the heat of the day, waiting and listening for the inevitable wreck and smuggling stories to surface. Storms, secret passages, the Spanish galleon off Biggar, 'brandy for the parson, baccy for the clerk. . . .' As the evening wore on, the mind really took flight.

CROSSING THE SANDS

There is no doubt that from earliest times, the vista, at low water, of what appeared to be continuous sand as far as the Lake District mountains tempted travellers to choose this route instead of the daunting prospect of 20 miles north towards Kendal and then 20 miles south-west to Cartmel and Furness. Between were areas of marsh and forest not to mention hills. However, to venture the quicker route, especially without a guide, was to court disaster.

What was known as the Cross Sands route, Hest Bank to Kents Bank, varied between 8 and 12 miles. Of the rivers flowing into Morecambe Bay there were fords at low water – the River Kent had three – Foulshaw to Sandside, Meathop to Arnside, and Kent's Bank to Silverdale. Until 1974 Furness and Cartmel, then part of Lancashire, were known as 'Lonsdale North of the Sands'.

Records show that foolhardy 'chancing it' led to many deaths. The job of guide was held within certain families for generations, but there was hardship for them. In 1928 two rushcutters, Thomas Houghton and Henry Bradley, were drowned while crossing the Sands. At the beginning of the eighteenth century a horse and a man, well-preserved, were suddenly exposed and at the same time three men with their horses were lost on Ulverston Sands.

A petition from guides (at one time three guides were necessary to take over at different points) stated that John Carter, in 1715, asked for more money as he 'had to keep two horses summer and winter and attend the eddy for four miles upon Sands, twelve hours in every twenty-four . . . he undergoes great hardship by exposure by wind and cold and being very wet, he by seeking out new fords every variation of the eddy and upon happenings of fogs and mists is put in danger of his life'.

Devil's Bridge at Kirkby Lonsdale is in an area once known as 'Lonsdale, North of the Sands'.

William Benson, Sands Guide, c. 1995. William is holding a giant jellyfish, an interesting specimen found on one of his trips. He has a vehicle designed for the job and takes parties over the expanse of the sands in Morecambe Bay when the tide is out.

Between the sixteenth and nineteenth centuries 145 people were drowned. Cartmel Priory paid 'the carter': the first named Edmondson (1500). In 1535 it was William Gate. In these days Conishead Priory has responsibility for the Levens Guide, John Harley. 'Priests' Keer' was named after the monks of Cartmel Priory and referred to a large heap of stones in sand.

By 1758 a coach took over and Annals of Cartmel (Stockdale) reports that two long coaches, holding thirteen inside and a heavy load of luggage, passed through Flookburgh every day except Saturday but these heavy loads stuck in sands and were replaced by lighter kinds. A July 1854 advertisement mentions 'the Rapid Oversands Coach will run on Sundays, outside 4s, inside 6s, leaving Lancaster at 2.45 p.m.' The Guides laid out 'brogs' or large twigs as signs to follow but channels changed rapidly and the approach to Furness, before the days of the railways, made crossing by Lancaster and Ulverston extremely hazardous. Rivers Kent and Keer were particularly dangerous. A useful Cross Sands 'marker' was the copper smelter chimney at Jenny

Brown's Point. Landmarks or places of refuge were proposed and subscriptions solicited by Mr Charles Seward who issued a description. 'It consists of four wooden pillars supporting a platform above High Water Mark accessible by steps of iron. A bell will be placed at the top, rung by wind or tide as a guide to all travellers.' However quicksands and shifting channels made this idea not a great success.

The Kent channels could be so deep that the horses were up to their shoulders in water. On reaching dry land it was a case of forging on through Allithwaite, Flookburgh, Cark and Cartmel.

A coach across the Sands, around 1830, covered the 7 miles from Hest Bank to Kents Bank, 2 miles north of Humphrey Head, the bay being washed by tide twice in every twenty-four hours. Travellers, who went on from Kent's Bank to Furness, would wait to cross over Leven Sands for another twelve hours. Waiting for the tide was beneficial for the innkeepers, especially at Flookburgh where there were many inns.

John Wesley noticed this when he did the crossing and said, 'I advise no stranger to go this way' and he passed over four sands, Duddon and Ravenglass adding to the dangers. Talking to Cedric Robinson who does the job so efficiently now, we both felt the utmost respect for his courage and his selflessness. Cedric takes parties between Hest Bank and Kents Bank, which is close to Guides Farm where he lives. He manages his smallholding, understands cockling and leads a pet donkey to the local old people's home every Christmas to delight. At our last visit Cedric was nursing a pigeon back to health. The bird was managing very well on its one leg. Truly a man of many parts.

Low tide, c. 1880. Kent estuary cocklers set off, passing Kent Steers.

WILLIAM HUTTON AND DAUGHTER CATHERINE CROSS THE SANDS

In crossing the Sands, the Kent estuary was the main obstacle because it could change course and alter channels. Holme Island near Grange-over-Sands was sometimes in Lancashire or sometimes in Westmorland, depending on how the River Kent flowed. A causeway to the island was eventually built.

An 1850 description of the scene crossing to Hest Bank 'looked like a caravan crossing the Arabian Desert . . . oxen, sheep, horsemen, fishermen, carriers, chaises, gigs, coaches'. The famous painter J.M.W. Turner captured the scene on canvas. Prayers were said by a priest 'for those who crossed the Sands with ebb of morning tide' (William Wordsworth). One among them was that great walker William Hutton who 'did' the Lakes in 1801 and stayed at Hest Bank. At the age of seventy-seven he set out from his home in Birmingham and walked to the Lake District. He was a successful printer and writer. Among his works was *The History of the Roman Wall*. He was usually accompanied by his daughter, Catherine, whom we much thank for recording William's observations in the prefaces to his books. Catherine, riding pillion, lodged at inns to meet up with her father, one of these meeting places being Hest Bank on 12 July 1801.

They agreed to pay the innkeeper 5s 'and some grog' if he took them across the Sands. Before crossing the River Kent with their little cart 'and a small horse which

Grange-over-Sands. 'A scattering of mansions, cottages and odds and ends of streets', pictured a century ago when port trade was killed off and tourist trade took over to make Grange the 'Torquay of the North'.

had almost learned to live without eating' to their relief, having become wary of the innkeeper's skills, they met the official guide to the Sands. The guide told the Huttons that with the coming of the stagecoaches his income had gone down as travellers attached themselves to the coaches. The landlord relied on the marks of the coach wheels, which were soon washed away by the next tide!

Hutton passed through Cartmel and Newby Bridge, and then in his indefatigable style walked the length of Windermere. Catherine reveals that he ate well, shunned alcoholic drink, rose at 4 a.m. and together they visited Belle Isle and dined at Bowness. 'The pace did not even fatigue his shoes. He walked 600 miles in one pair and scarcely made a hole in his stockings.'

Catherine returned to Hest Bank to await her father's return but on went William through Ambleside, Kirkstone, Penrith and through to Carlisle! He returned via Kendal, then on to Hest Bank to meet his daughter who was regaled with the sad story of how the Roman wall was being despoiled. One farmer had taken enough stone to build himself a farmhouse. William had requested Mr Tulip to desist or he would wound the whole body of antiquaries by putting an end to the most noble antiquity in the whole island . . . 'By easy marches I arrived at Birmingham on 7 August 1801 after a loss of one stone in weight, forty guineas, thirty-five days and a walk of 601 miles.'

Eddie and I would have liked to have met this extraordinary man and take him to the source of the River Kent on High Street but we were two and a half centuries too late and we would never have been able to keep up with him! For goodness sake, he was seventy-seven! From his daughter's account of this enterprise it is plain that he had a wry sense of humour. What a wonderful companion with whom to go fell-walking. We were glad he rejoiced so much in the marvellous scenery.

10

Over the Sea to Fell Countree

What became known as 'The Barrow Boats' for years and years gave immense pleasure to thousands of people. In 1904, every weekday during August and September, there were three trips to Barrow-in-Furness and three back to Fleetwood at the unbelievable return fare of 2*s*, or 3*s* if travelling saloon. Season tickets were even bigger bargains, with a possible seventy-two trips for only £2. The best-loved paddle steamers were *Lady Evelyn*, *Lady Moyra* and *Lady Margaret*, leading up to a Grand Circular Tour in wagonettes.

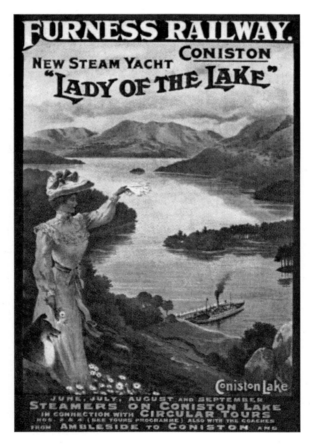

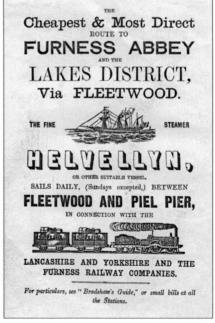

'The cheapest and most direct route to Furness Abbey'. Steam yacht Lady of the Lake – from Ambleside to Coniston and Greenodd to Lake Bank.

Furness Railway, '20 Rail, Coach and Steam Yacht Tours' poster. The season lasted from 1 May to 30 September.

Lady Margaret left Fleetwood at 10.30 a.m, and arrived at Ramsden Dock, Barrow, at 11.45 a.m. Here passengers could catch a train for Lakeside, Windermere, which would arrive at 12.50 p.m. For those desirous of even more travel the natural follow-on was a steamer trip to Ambleside or the cheaper 'Inner Tour' costing 4s 9d. This included a visit to Furness Abbey and a gondola trip on Lake Coniston. In all, this lasted ten hours, the paddle steamer returning for Fleetwood at 7 p.m.

Furness Railway, represented by secretary and general manager Alfred Aslett, offered a great deal, impeccably organised. From 1 May to 30 September: 'Twenty Rail, Coach and Steam Yacht Tours' embraced Windermere, Grasmere, Thirlmere, Coniston, Ullswater, Wastwater etc. with visits to Furness Abbey and the home of the famous painter George Romney, in Kendal. Trips also ran from Greenodd.

'Furness Abbey and the Lake District' had attracted tourists from as early as 1840 when the coming of the railway had made such trips possible. In those days, when arrangements were nothing like so well organised, the steamer Helvellyn, from all accounts an old tub, sailed daily to Piel Pier and would-be passengers were roused by the bell man. Landings at Piel and Bardsea were unpredictable and from thence to Conishead it was a case of 'all jammed together in a two-horse car, precious bone-shaking affairs they are as I learned to my discomfort last autumn . . . in spite of bumps and thumps we all enjoyed the lovely view.' (1842).

In the early twentieth century trippers from all over Lancashire availed themselves of Mr Aslett's excellent facilities. He worked with Messrs Thomas Cook & Son who had produced a free pamphlet, 'Tours through Lake Land'. That enterprising firm, Sankeys of Barrow, was on board the paddle steamers to photograph groups, the souvenir photographs being ready for collection when it was time to steam back home after a grand day out.

Ed J. Burrow issued a series of penny guides on the *Abbeys of Old England*. Armed with the one on Furness Abbey, the keen traveller had a treat in store: a full illustrated history plus further information on the chief characteristics of the five styles of ecclesiastical architecture, all for 1*d*. I remember hearing my grandfather describe the whole brochure as 'staggering value for money'.

Furness Abbey Hotel, then under the management of H.P. Stephenson, was advertised as 'one of the ideal hotels of the United Kingdom'. It certainly had some unique characteristics: the original bas-reliefs of Italian workmanship, marble-framed in black oak, exquisitely carved, from the abbey. These had become the principal

Furness Abbey, c. 1860.

features of 'the Abbot's Room, a sitting room complete with ecclesiastical stained glass'. 'The favourite resort of the Artist, Antiquary, and lover of the Picturesque' adjoined Furness Abbey station by covered approach. Through carriages ran to London Euston, Liverpool, Leeds and Bradford. All-inclusive weekend terms, from dinner on Saturday evening to breakfast on Monday morning cost just one guinea. Back home, stony broke, if you had to drink Fry's cocoa for the rest of the week it was only 4½*d* for a quarter pound tin in those days.

If the weather was unpropitious the crossing from Fleetwood to Barrow could be very rough and there are some harrowing accounts, but, in the main, people from all walks of life sang its praises, revelling in the sea air and, apart from Barrow docks, the magnificent scenery from start to finish. John Stuart Mill loved it, although he had only hard words for Blackpool and Fleetwood: 'they are but ugly places'. This is a view shared by an unknown curate in 1844, who gave a eulogistic account of the sea voyage: 'Morecambe Bay, in which we sailed the steamer, was enough to put one in good heart again for it was a lovely morning. . . . Far away rolled the Irish Ocean and on our near side rose one behind the other the mountains . . . Coniston Old Man in the distance.' Of the abbey he writes: 'A more perfect ruin I have never seen . . . . a place never to be effaced from my memory as it is not only with recollections of its own grandeur, but with those of other scenes which I have witnessed during that trip. Had I a hundred tongues I could not find words to express my astonishment, admiration and almost veneration. . . .' This lucky young man, who also displays a nice sense of humour and an appreciation of the Furness home brew, was writing at the very dawn of the railway age and indeed of the age of tourism itself. It is not surprising that there were many sad hearts and faces when, because of the imminent war, this highly successful service had to be suspended in 1913.

When Eddie and I started our jaunts into Kentmere, sailings to the jumping-off places for Cumbrian fells were long a thing of the past. What a wonderful day out it must have been! Sea air, mountain air, a sail on a lake, a rowing boat on a river, plus ecclesiastical air if you toured Furness Abbey, not to mention riding in a high wagonette. All for 4s 9d. Bargains do not come better than that.

COUNTY BOUNDARIES AND STEAMERS

The Local Government Boundary Commission altered the confines of some counties so radically that a quarter of a century later many people are still not reconciled to their decisions. Southport, for example, dislikes being classed as Merseyside. We mourn the loss of areas of beautiful countryside, once Lancashire, which have passed to what is now known as Cumbria but which, when we were young, were called Cumberland and Westmorland.

Before 1974, Windermere's Lakeside and part of Coniston were in Lancashire, visited by tourists from all over the country with great enjoyment. A lucky few motored up in the early days of road travel. Recently one octogenarian told me: 'We had a bull-nosed Morris and used to go via Garstang. We would picnic on the slope by Keppel Bridge and put a big stone behind one of the car wheels.'

'We are sailing', not to Rod Stewart country but not far off. Eddie and Catherine off to the Isle of Man on Snae Fell, summer 1989.

As early as the eighteenth century tourists were discovering the beauty. Thomas Gray's Journal in the Lakes was an early guide, written for a sick friend he had to leave behind at Brough. Gray made his descriptions particularly vivid in order to heighten the visual impact. For those who could afford the time and money to travel so far north, Gray laid out a wealth of routes, vantage points, inns and not-to-be-missed views. No motors then, just unmetalled tracks and packhorse routes.

In 1874 William Black drove a lurching, swaying phaeton for his London friends, drawn by two jet-black horses, Castor and Pollux. Windermere, with its 'wilderness of water, wind and sky', impressed them most, but at Lakeside and Newby Bridge they were shocked to see 'young ladies, tarred and feathered, with staring stripes and alarming petticoats, men wearing comical jackets and knickerbockers'. Bright braces, alpenstocks and leather trousers abounded at the hotels quickly set up to receive those early crowds. It was in that year that Richard Rigg commenced his service of 'Rigg's Royal Mail and other Coaches'.

The fame of John Ruskin, great Victorian art critic, inevitably added to the tourist industry. He lived at Brantwood, Coniston for thirty years and enjoyed sails from his home. Possibly early tourists looked over the wall to catch a glimpse of the great man sitting in his rock-hewn chair in the garden, where he wrote *The Stones of Venice*.

Sea routes linked with the railways meant that by 1847 the steamer *Helvellyn* was taking passengers from Fleetwood. For a second-class return fare of *3s* passengers arrived at Barrow for 7.30 a.m. from where they went on to Furness, Windermere, Lakeside or Coniston. For those with horses and carriages Lieutenant Edward Robinson's steamer *The Express* was just right. So were the fares:

Four-wheeled carriages £1 10*s*
Two-wheeled carriages £1
Horses 10*s*
Dogs 1*s*
20 sheep £1

The Express sailed via Bardsea. The Giant Circular Tour (*7s 6d* outer, *5s 6d* inner) took in magnificent scenery: Windermere, Coniston, Furness Abbey, Cartmel Priory, Grange and Newby Bridge. Spears and Pond provided luncheons and teas on board the paddle steamer *Lady Margaret* and, as popularity increased, there were more steam yachts and gondolas, some with a German band on board.

To reach Lakeside, passengers travelled that stretch of line once used by H.W. Schneider, the ironmaster who resided at Belsfield House, now The Belsfield Hotel,

Lakeside station from where the steamers Swan and Teal depart.

Major Dennis Smith and Mollie, his wife, 'swanning' with a resident outside the Belsfield Hotel, Bowness-on-Windermere. The Belsfield was once the home of the famous ironmaster, John Wilkinson, who came after H.W. Schneider.

Bowness. Every morning on board his private steam yacht, *Esperance*, servants prepared his breakfast in great style. Amid an array of glittering silver and cut glass he consumed coffee and devilled kidneys while sailing the six miles of Windermere before entraining first class for Barrow-in-Furness.

Before the Campbells broke water speed records there, the long, lean stretch of Coniston Water was already known for its most famous craft, the *Gondola*, launched in 1859. Noted for its luxurious interior decoration like a royal railway carriage, it was designed by Furness Railway chief James Ramsden and built by Jones and

Quiggan of Liverpool. Felix Hammill, a married man with nine children, was its best-known captain. He made 13,000 sailings without mishap. In 1906 *Gondola* carried 23,000 passengers. Thomas Carlyle and John Ruskin sailed in her and Arthur Ransome of Swallows and Amazons fame used her as the model for Captain Flint's houseboat. Traditionally, every season ended with the long, wailing whistle of *Gondola*'s farewell echoing across the lake.

In the eighty years of her passenger-cruising *Gondola* was said to burn a bag of coke on each round trip. When the Second World War broke out her engine and boiler went to power a sawmill in Ulverston, so she was used simply as a houseboat with concrete in the hull to stabilise her, but even worse was to follow. Thirty years later she was wrecked in a storm and became derelict. Happily, after much hard work and fundraising, the queen of the lake has returned to active service on Coniston Water and can again be boarded in what is one of the most beautiful areas in Cumbria.

In the partition, Lancashire lost not only magnificent tracts of the world's finest scenery, but farming ways of life, crafts such as charcoal burning, quaint place names and age old traditions. No wonder some counties are clamouring to regain what they consider to be rightly theirs from time immemorial!

Launched on Coniston Water in 1859, Gondola *served until 1937. The National Trust have restored this graceful craft which can carry eighty-six passengers.*

A Priory and Two Chapels Among the Fells

As a schoolboy, Eddie attended Hutton Grammar School where he became captain of cricket and captain of rugby. One Easter we had been regaled by stories of Captain Bagot's cricket XI in 1892, so it was interesting stuff and quite novel to hear about the wheelbarrows of radishes as part of refreshments. The last survivor of the eleven by the River Kent was Henry Walker of Brettargh Hall, not far distant from Levens.

Once again we had Arnside Knott in our sights and the prospect from its summit over the shining waters of the Kent estuary proved perfect. Low green hills, silvery limestone scars and purple hazy fells swooned off into that distance once known as Lonsdale, North of the Sands. While the weather lasted we went to seek again the peace of the Vale of Cartmel, a name derived from 'caer' (camp) and 'meol' (sandbank). Camden tells us that in 677 the king of Northumberland 'gave the land of Cartmell and all the Britons in it to Cuthbert, Bishop of Lindisfarne'. Lands were conveyed and he probably raised a church witnessed by monks or high-ranking clerics at Cartmell, the name itself losing an 'L' as the years advanced.

A legend attached to the priory tells how a group of monks, searching for water and the best site, discovered twin streams crossing each other. A sign, they decided, and there they must build their church. Between the stream running north and the other south, upon St Bernard's Mount arose Cartmell Priory. History, not legend records that building commenced in 1188, the precincts extending over twenty-two

Cartmel Priory, c. 1900.

The old gateway at Cartmel, now National Trust property, which led to the Cavendish Arms in 1960, was all that was left, apart from the Church of the Augustinian Priory, dating from 1330. From 1624 to 1790 the building above the gateway served as a grammar school. Among many ancient and interesting relics at Cartmel Priory are copies of Spenser's Faerie Queene of 1596, a 1503 black leather Bible in six volumes and a folio copy of Foxe's Book of Martyrs. There is also an ancient umbrella, one of the finest of its kind.

acres. In the centre of Cartmel Village the old gateway can still be seen. Re-modelled in the fourteenth and fifteenth centuries, a new belfry tower was placed diagonally on the early, low lantern of the priory thus creating what is possibly a unique feature. The hallowed sense of peace this beautiful building within the fells can evoke is also for some people, unique and Easter Day 1971 was a perfect time to attend service there. We came out bathed in sunshine.

That part of Morecambe Bay and the River Kent itself, flanked by rolling fells and valleys, seems to cut off the busy world. High along the peat mosses we entered a special part of Cumbrian country. Here the Quakers built their cottage-style Height Chapel 600ft above sea level in 1677, probably as a direct result of George Fox's preaching. He was connected with Swarthmoor, near Ulverston. The isolation of The Height was selected as safer for a persecuted group. These people suffered for what they sincerely believed. A small window over the porch was used as a lookout where a watcher could warn the congregation of approaching aggression. Not far

The Height, the Quakers' Meeting House on Cartmel Fell, 1908. It was built in 1677 after the commencement of the ministry of George Fox, who married the widow of Judge Fell of Swarthmoor near Ulverston. At the time of this photograph, taken by Mr Holmes of Ulverston, the meeting house, with its own burial ground attached, had a female sexton who lived in the adjoining village. The chapel had a watchtower above the porch, as the Quakers had to be on their guard against rough handling by people who opposed them. Fines were imposed upon Quakers at the slightest excuse and persecution drove them to remote spots miles from any town. The golden sands of Morecambe Bay are visible from here and 600ft below lie the Holker peat mosses and Hilton Tarn.

distant from The Height, George Fox himself was pitched over a high wall by an angry mob. His wife, the widow of Judge Fell of Swarthmoor, regularly attended the Meeting House. Her disciplined ways and Spartan style extended particularly to the younger women. Finery and self-aggrandisement had no place at The Height Chapel.

St Anthony's chapel at Cartmel Fell (this saint being 'patron of the wilds and the woods') gave distant views of the Howgill Fells. Severe storms in 1893 felled its fir trees. The site, although not so bleak as Height Chapel, was open to all the winds that blew. Worshippers arrived on horseback so a mounting-block with central stake for tethering steeds was necessary in the middle of the churchyard.

St Anthony was also the patron saint of basket makers (swills) and charcoal burners. The arms of the barons of Kendal blazed from stained glass but there was no seating. A hermitage with its own chapel was probably set up by the Priory of Cartmel as a hospice for travellers. According to Nicholson's History, there was no road over Cartmel Fell in 1770.

11

Chain Ferries, Ancient Fords and Coaching Days

Cunsey Ferry was fun but we enjoyed crossing Lake Windermere by the chain ferry not far from Bowness in rain and shine throughout all seasons of the year. Our thoughts often turn to storms on the lake and to the days when carriages, not cars, were carried; to that incident in the nineteenth century when a wedding party, worse for drink, was returning on the ferry and their wagonette overturned, drowning horses and passengers in the lake.

The chain ferry, c. 1900. When Thomas Sleddale was Mayor of Kendal it was reported one October, that the River Kent 'rose into the church vestry and on the day following 48 men and women and 9 horses were drowned in Windermere water by the upsetting of a boat having been at a wedding'. This wagonette party is crossing the river by ferry in 1904. The horses had to be soothed by an experienced handler during the crossing.

Some of the Rothwell family prior to catching the chain ferry, at the south end of
Windermere Shore, 1996. Eddie is seated by the water.

Lake District packhorse tracks and turnpike roads have an interesting history. Before the turnpike road to Milnthorpe was opened in 1819, apart from the dangerous over-Sands route there was only one road leading from Cartmel Fells area. The way was from Ulverston to Kendal by Penny Bridge, Newby Bridge, Gummers How and Crosthwaite, but this road fell into such ruinous state, that an Act of Parliament was sought. It took 111 years' collection of tolls from those who used the new route to pay for the turnpike road that followed.

At the southern end of Windermere the lack of roads could mean a long trek via Newby Bridge but country folk used two fords across the lake, their long, colourful history being arguably even more interesting than that of the tracks and roads.

The first ancient ford was about a mile from Newby Bridge, the second opposite Fell Foot. A tradition that a 'tinkler', as tinkers were known in the Lake District, had drowned in crossing by the first, earned it the name of Tinkler's Ford. The unfortunate man was found standing upright, immovably planted in mud, his pack still on his back. He had strayed off the direct ford line into Dog Tarn, thought at one time to be unfathomable with a whirlpool at the bottom. The shelving, muddy side of the hole (its other name was Dog Hole) held the tinker fast.

Mr and Mrs Tyson in their orchard with sheepdog Nip, Kentdale, late nineteenth century.

Lord of the Isles *is on the right of this photograph, beached. The steam yacht* Lady of the Lake *is afloat, Newby Bridge,* c. 1870.

Lady of the Lake, *a new version ready for launching, 1872.*

Fell Foot Ford, 55yds long, was only 3ft deep under normal conditions and strewn with large boulders, one of these known as the Cheese Press. This acted as a guide to water depth, for waders knew that if the Cheese Press was covered they must turn back and proceed to Newby Bridge. It also marked the position of the Bass Hole, a treacherous 8ft deep hole nearby. These boulders were a help to the people fording but a nuisance to the barges bringing slate from Langdale and other quarries. On return journeys, carrying lime from Field Broughton, the bargees cast overboard a small part of the cargo as their guide to the safest passage when they came next time.

When roads were suitable for wagonettes and other wheeled vehicles, trains of packhorses were no longer used and the fords fell into disuse. In 1895 at Newby Bridge the first steamboat, *Lady of the Lake*, was built and a 5ft deep passage was cleared between both fords. Five of the huge boulders, which had probably been there since the Ice Age, were dragged away by chains and heavy horses to the Landing How shore, among them the hoary Cheese Press, its useful days to forders of the lake over, but in its time seen by drovers, pilgrims, packmen, monks, Romans, friars, parsons, soldiers, farmers, labourers, miners, housewives, children, ponies, dogs and other animals.

The photograph opposite below shows steamship *Lady of the Lake* at Newby Bridge in 1872. It was interesting to find out that the Chain Ferry at Bowness, which we used when we were exploring Claife Heights, was made at the old Dock Yard in Dock Road, Lytham, not far from where we lived.

A troupe of Victorian ladies on an outing, having travelled on the steamer Helvellyn. They are outside the ruins of Furness Abbey, and Mrs Fanny Jameson is second from the left, 1860.

Horse-drawn traffic appeals to Cumbrian tourists, Bowness, 1989.

COACHING DAYS

The Lake District Herald Book Shop, Ambleside and inns throughout Kentdale displayed a splendid poster with the timetable for 'Rigg's Royal Mail and Other Coaches', which ran between Windermere and Keswick. Richard Rigg started the service in 1847 when the railway was brought to Windermere and, as demand increased, he extended it. Well-established as livery and jobmaster, Mr Brown of the Queen's Hotel, Ambleside also provided a coach but long before either, the Flying Machine drawn by six horses, with postilions astride the two leaders, set off from the King's Arms, Kendal, on a journey to London which took three days. Speed not being of the essence, they averaged 6 miles an hour! By 1793 the North Mail was covering Kendal to Carlisle in six hours and the Carlisle Post to London, also a journey of three days, charged £3 10s fare. Towards the end of the nineteenth century, for visitors from Rigg's Hotel, Windermere, to travel with the driver on top of the private coach, luggage between, cost 7s, but to travel inside was 9s 6d.

Quite the best known local service, Rigg's endured until 1920 and in its time carried some renowned passengers: Dr Arnold to his home, Foxe Howe in Ambleside; Felicia Hemans; John Stuart Mill: Harriet Martineau: John Ruskin; Sir Henry Acland. The scientist Dr John Dalton often visited Jonathan Otley, clock maker and author of the first comprehensive Lakes Guide, who lived in a tiny cottage up a flight of stone steps in King's Yard, Keswick. Jonathan, a self-taught scientist, discussed his theories on Derwentwater's floating island with the famous atomic-theory scientist, who would on occasions be accompanied by equally famous friends, all of whom probably travelled in the coach.

Drawn by four horses, with the coachmen wearing grey top hats, Rigg's Royal Mail Coaches were a splendid sight. 'Just before starting', wrote Edmund Blogg in 1898, 'there is the usual bustle, so dear to the hearts of coachmen and grooms. The horn is sounded, all passengers are seated, the driver tightens the reins and we are rattling over the stony street.'

Travelling from Keswick to Windermere through some of the most beautiful scenery in the world, on a clear fine day, what an exhilarating run it would be with the trumpeting of the Yard of Tin, as the coach horn was then known, echoing through the passes whenever the stage approached a stop. One such was outside Rigg's Windermere Hotel, in the days when the old drinking fountain was situated in the middle of the road. In Ambleside, coaches halted at the door of the Queen's Hotel.

The Ullswater coach that was pulled to the top of Kirkstone Pass climbed 1,476ft. Among G.P. Abraham's series of vintage comic postcards is a reference to the 'Four-horse shay', which took tourists over Honister Pass. The sepia postcard was endorsed:

> This painful truth, experience will tell,
> It's mostly, walk and pay your fare as well.

Able-bodied passengers often had to get out and walk over Dunmail Raise, but few minded and one young curate, travelling in 1847, wrote: 'Perhaps there have been few better ways of looking at mountains as one leans back to the clop of hooves.'

The new railway companies worked in close conjunction with such hoteliers as Richard Rigg, but sometimes there was not a seat to be had. The Revd Charles A. Tryon, in his Lakeland tour, wrote in his diary, 'Picked up my carpet bag and waited for the Carlisle Mail to Lancaster but found it crowded inside and out, so contented myself with thoughts of staying another day.' At Ambleside he had been driven 'in some style in a two-horse car with postilion in yellow jacket . . . Oh, the pleasure of going downhill, bump, jump, all of a lump.'

When Rigg's Coach Service was withdrawn in 1920 the omnibuses of the Lake District Road Traffic Company replaced it. In the name of progress, yet another colourful Lake District tradition passed into history.

HIGH FLIER FROM BOWNESS

At Hill of Oaks on the south-west shore of Windermere Lake between Bowness and Newby Bridge, in the last four months of 1911, 'a wonderful machine', having at last been constructed, was undergoing trials. A former mayor of Kendal, Captain Edward William Wakefield, pioneer in the art of flying from water, had invested

£3,000 in the venture, which also involved the 5th Earl, Lord Lonsdale, and pilot H. Stanley Adams, holder of the Aero Club's certificate. The race was on for the best invention. Such a satisfactory test flight of the hydro aeroplane Waterhen had been accomplished that a reporter from the Westmorland Gazette was invited to witness the second test flight to take place on Monday 2 December 1911. Confidence was high and proved justified. Of the very few spectators, workman Mr Candlish of Michigan, then living at Merewood, south of the Low Wood Hotel, maintained, 'I have seen nothing to surpass the test on Windermere'.

The most conspicuous feature of the two-decked aeroplane was its Gnome 50hp engine with seven shining cylinders and the 8ft 6in Roe propellor with mahogany blades capable of over 1,000 revolutions per minute. A foot lever up front controlled the rudder. A framework of silver spruce and bamboo was strengthened by hickory wood at the site of the engine and petrol tank, quite the heaviest part of the whole equipment. Vibration, which was prodigious, was cushioned and dispersed by rubber. Once the hydro aeroplane got going, escaping exhaust gases showed up like a colourful firework display in the fading light of that grey December day. Waterhen hoped to improve on the many aeroplane trials by running over and alighting on water. To achieve this a longitudinal, watertight chamber of aluminium, mahogany and canvas, designed like a float, was attached to the plane by successive pairs of strong stays. Adding further equilibrium were two balanced cylinders filled with air, the total weight of the whole outfit including the pilot being about 700lb.

The *Westmorland Gazette* observer was impressed: 'The plane was brought from the berth, did the two courses on the water and the two circuits in the air and returned safe and sound to the hangar in the space of 40 minutes.' After two years of constant experiment, enquiry and observation, the descent was beautifully bird-like, the whole display prompt, uninterrupted and smooth. Flying at an altitude of 40 to 50ft, pilot Adams covered 2 miles, but it was apparent that Ambleside and back would have been well within Waterhen's scope.

So far as then known, Mr Wakefield was the first man in Westmorland to build a flying machine which had actually got into the air, covered a prescribed course and returned to its quarters without mishap, indeed the first man in England to build a successful hydro aeroplane and demonstrate its success. Two years previously, near Marseilles, a Frenchman, Henri Fabre, had some initial successes but sadly his machine was reported as 'not to fly very well'. The Swiss lakes, the Pacific coast and the River Seine all saw experimentation in sustained flight. Around the shores of Windermere alone were a number of attempts, all adding to revolutionary experiments that were later to prove valuable in the design of seaplanes and flying boats. Captain Adams' flight on that grey, drizzly December day was 'a distinction for Windermere' but not all were so fortunate.

Mr Grosspelius, whose experiments drew officers from HMS *Hermione*, based at Barrow, hoping to incorporate hydroplanes as an accessory to warships, made an ignominious showing. For months this gentleman from Silver Holme, Graythwaite had also been experimenting with a hydro aeroplane berthed at Messrs Borwicks'

The trials of the hydro-aeroplane Waterhen, *1911.*

boathouses. On one of his trial trips, 'perched on the elevated seat in front', he set off at a great rate towards the ferry but within a minute the craft swerved sharply to right and to left. Portions of the propeller flew high into the air and the plane somersaulted, flinging the pilot into Lake Windermere near Cockshott. A motorboat sped to his rescue but the undaunted Mr Grosspelius was, in no time, superintending salvage. A broken propeller and wing caused two weeks' delay, all due to an unexpectedly strong gust of wind; his second mishap in his second hydro aeroplane!

'If at first you don't succeed, try, try, try again' must have been the watchword by which these intrepid innovators worked. Disappointment acted as a spur to ambition, but perhaps there was something in the Westmorland air as well.

12

Ever Rolling Streams

Rivers, streams, tarns and estuaries are inspiring and great writers and thinkers have left us their words and thoughts about them: William Shakespeare, Edmund Spenser, who begged 'Sweet Thames run softly', the Romans, who worshipped the River Severn 'Sabrina fair' and the poet Drayton, who loved the sylvan Wyre.

Rivers Kent, Sprint, Mint and Bela had similar effects on us as we grew to know them in all weathers and various conditions. There were panting hot summer days, cold icy days in snow and rain, days of roaring wind that tossed trees and tore at the rivers banks, but the days when grey, dismal non-stop drizzle penetrated even

A Westmorland brass band. Not the Festival Jazzmen, but worthy counterparts more than a century ago. Brass bands were indispensable for most occasions. Some accompanied visitors on board the lake steamers.

Eddie and Catherine on one of the K-K-K-Katy trips. Here we are at Grasmere on our way to Keswick up from Kendal. The snow looked marvellous but was melting fast in the bright sunshine. A Christmas trip – and perhaps an advertisement for Grenfell anoraks.

Grenfell anoraks we gave up and retreated to the car. Such a one was when we abandoned the notion of reaching Helsington Snuff Mill on Kent's banks until weather improved. Paths were being turned into streams, misty fells steel blue-grey and the River Kent in its rocky areas became a crashing, white torrent.

Our boots stormed rocky outcrops, waded through dubs, squelched through sedge, peat hags, sucking tussocks and snagging furze. Not a soul did we meet. Rarely did we give up for weather can change suddenly, bringing nice surprises as well as gloom.

'Out in the wilds and over the tops to Kentmere', was a photograph we found in a junk shop in winter 1982. Together we pounced on it.

Back at the car I would scribble my attempts at poetry, bits of verse, while Eddie busied himself working on jazz programmes for forthcoming 'gigs'. The Festival Jazzmen for whom he wrote up, prior to going to press, their performances at concerts, frequently played at Newby Bridge or Backbarrow, possibly Kendal.

Only once was this head of English inspired by the muse to write verse, so Eddie's rhyming couplets, when rained off, take pride of place. The streams of consciousness left behind by Virginia Woolf flowed to me. Many times we climbed Arnside Knott and on that particular day just about everything was as perfect as I remember it now. It's hardly Michael Palin, but it seemed to epitomise our whole venture.

'THE FESTIVAL OF JAZZMEN'S LAMENT'

(with apologies to Stanley Holloway, Dave Howitt et al.)

When arrangements were made for the local parade
To be led by a famous brass band,
No one thought it quite fair that the hard-working mayor
Should deliver the letter by hand.

So to make quite a hit one inscrutable twit
Thought he'd pulled off a masterful trick
And persuade Cyril Wroe he should stand up and blow
With his seven-piece jazz band plus Vic.

And so it transpired that the Jazzmen were hired
For an undisclosed generous fee,
In good weather or bad to play marches and trad,
Not to treat the whole thing as a spree.

But they never decided should wheels be provided
To transport the amps and the drum,
So imagine the job when Geoff, Ronnie and Bob
Had to balance it all on their tum.

On that glorious day they all started to play,
By the splendid occasion inspired,
But in spite of strong will, at the top of the hill
With three choruses each they felt tired.

But once over the crest, they regained all their zest,
The momentum now driving them on.
They went faster and faster to total disaster.
Tempo, balance and rhythm all gone.

'They can't march to the beat of our South Rampart Street,'
Shouted Cyril, now blinded by sun.
'If we don't slow it down when we get near the town
They'll all roll up their shirt sleeves and run.'

With a push from the rear, a trombone in his ear
And his trumpet he said wasn't cheap,
Derek went up a tone, sat on Vic's vibraphone,
And the whole band collapsed in a heap.

Not to mention the name of the one they should blame,
But to save what they could from the wreck,
And to maintain the peace, they all tried to release
The punctured drum skin from Geoff's neck.

But this amiable gent wasn't quick to relent
After being so roughly misused,
And to strike up again with the Festival Men
With a gesture he flatly refused.

'Geoff, Geoff pick up thy drum stick,'
They pleaded, alas, but in vain.
'No! Tha knocked it down, so tha picks it up,'
Wailed the drummer again and again.

So to settle the peace with a speedy release
From this impasse by plain common sense,
Cyril spoke to the band, put the stick in Geoff's hand
And proclaimed, 'Now let battle commence!'

Edwin G. Rothwell

ARNSIDE KNOTT: A SUMMER SONG

See, quintessence of summer sealed in three jars.
The deep distilled purple of wild blackberries
Rakes memories of an unforgotten day;
The year fruit ripened early
Steeping in dews, sun-soaked at noon,
Parched earth, three months flung round its pulsing heat.

This year made magic in the woods and clearings,
Ladened the hedgerows,
Mingling bramble with gorse,
Heather, harebell, wild rose and campion.
Such tapestry as the weeks sped by
Harnessed to sunshine.

Climbing the Knott that day,
Summer sang in our veins.
We plucked ripe harvest, treading warily
As juices ran like wine.
Bruised velvet bled.
Thorns pierced our flesh unheeded,
Simply fuelling desire for more and more.
The sun, between our shoulder blades
Acted like fire to quicken.

Standing proud, pines busy with birdsong
Reached for the sky, echoing triumph.
Light winds sifted the silver birches all aloof
And Morecambe Bay, its infinite capacity
Shadowing the opal sea's end,
Lay silver brilliant, upturned like a shield,

So two tramps turned for home, a sweet release,
Licking their wounds indelible,
And bagged with riches.

We curtain velvet night, shut out the dark.
Cumbrian scones and bramble jelly for tea!
Gales lash the Bay to equinoctial fury.
High on the brackening Knott
Fox twitches in sandy earth,
Home, lair and burrow.
We share the song of summer.

Catherine Rothwell

I enshrined this incident in doggerel verse, trying to remember Tommy's Westmorland accent as passed down from Annie.

'EGG TOMMY'

Of Lakeland characters galore
It's Egg Tommy I adore,
For he shared his home with a hundred hens
And asked for nothing more.
They flew upstairs to bed with him
And roosted on the floor.

Great grandma said that Tommy was
As strong as any horse.
He carried his eggs in baskets,
Was descended from the Norse.
The hens were barricaded in
Whenever he left home,
And his moleskins stuffed with savings,
Enough to buy up Rome.

As Tommy fed his hens one day
A ragged man descends,
Opening his eyes in wide surprise,
So many feathered friends!
On t' chair backs, on t' piano,
On t ert' sofa in the hall –
Rag-bone man's revelation!
Was this a Chickens' Ball?

At this point the downpour ceased and the sun came out. Just as well!

13

Cumbrian Characters

A Cumbrian character whom I recall was Vivian Fisher who, for years, walked from his Keswick home to open and close the gate on the Ashness Bridge Road for motorists heading for Watendlath. He was a perfect gentleman. A flower painter in oils and on glass, he had met John Ruskin, some years later attending the great Victorian's funeral. He also knew T.H. Hall Caine, friend of the pre-Raphaelite painter, Dante Gabriel Rossetti. Vivian was at one time a postman delivering letters on the fells. Born 7 September in Lupton's Yard, he lived until he was ninety, subsisting on small change from visitors. He spent the winter walking, painting or reading his favourite poems by the River Greta.

Another eccentric and lovable man who lived into his eighties inhabited a cave on Castle Crag, Borrowdale in the summertime. He was known as Professor Milligan Dalton. Sometimes he acted as a guide on the fells for he loved the out-of-doors and was unmistakable in his Tyrolean hat, bare legs and ankles bound with wool.

Famous for climbing were the Abraham brothers, Ashley and George. They were professional photographers. There are 700 of their wonderful negatives, including climbers in action, now housed in Tullie House Museum, Carlisle. The portly Ashley (15st in weight) sometimes got stuck in chimneys amid rock faces. Traversing Colliers Climb on Scafell Crag, Ashley's shoulders and head were used as footholds. 'How not to climb' they described early days when a clothes line was their rope! But the taking of photographs in a high wind was more dangerous than climbing Napes Needle at the foot of the south-facing crag of Great Gable. The equipment weighed over 20lb. Together with their father, during intervals at their Magic Lantern slide shows, they played a rock xylophone – musical stones carefully chipped from the volcanic rocks of Skiddaw and Blencathra, to produce the right sound. The Abrahams' well-known premises in Lake Road, Keswick, were sold to George Fisher in 1967. How well I remember buying my first pair of Helvellyn walking boots from there!

There were characters among the men of the slate quarries. Moses sled-gait (Moses Rigg from Wasdale) was a Honister quarryman. Frequently the quarrymen had biblical names ('sled' means sledge and 'gait' means path). Starting from the top of Fleetwith, avoiding the steep drop to Seatoller, Moses' sled probably carried the best slate. Tales of smuggling hung round the quarrymen, but not Moses.

Professor Milligan Dalton, known as the Cave Man. His card read 'Professor of adventure, camping, mountain rapid shooting, rafting and hair breadth adventures'. He lived in a cave blasted out of the slate on Castle Crag, eating mainly wholemeal bread baked in a primitive oven.

The first recorded successful tourist attempt on Napes Needle was in 1886 by Mr Haskett-Smith who left his handkerchief behind to prove it. My late brother Edward W. Houghton, attempted it much later with friends George Coates and Alan Cixby.

At Seatoller House, incidentally, lived Moses Pepper, also a quarryman and a strict Rechabite. He worked his wife and daughters very hard and was known as the master of the most famous place of lodging in all Cumberland in 1895. The visitors' book sported such names as G.M. Trevelyan, Bertrand Russell and Geoffrey Winthrop Young. Climbing fever was at its height.

It is on record that a Cumberland farmer, Joseph Thompson, unhappy in his marriage after three years, sold his wife at Carlisle Market (7 April 1832). Round her neck he placed a straw halter labelled 'Serpent' but conceded that she could milk cows, make butter, read novels and scold the farm-workers. She was sold for 20s plus a Newfoundland dog! Now Joseph must have been a character although I do not know any more about him than this.

EGG TOMMY

Egg Tommy was a remarkable and eccentric Lake District character. Among a conglomeration of true individualists he was unmistakable. Never ill, since 1849 Egg Tommy had passed in and out of the houses of the district with regularity akin to clockwork. Two large baskets were suspended over his shoulders, one on his back and another on his chest. He could carry an incredible weight, for these baskets were stocked with more than a hundred eggs every time he left home. Trade was good, for Tommy's eggs could always be relied upon to be fresh, so he returned home with plenty of ready money in the ample pockets of his moleskin trousers. In the thirty years of his journeying to Bowness, together with money he had previously saved as a farm servant, he amassed £900, which was considered a tidy fortune over a century ago.

Tommy would never allow anyone to go into his house except his feathered friends, the hens, perhaps because they were the source of his income. An amusing story was told of an incident about twelve months before Tommy died. A rag collector from Kendal came up to the door, Tommy having for once neglected to fasten his garden gate. The ragman's eyes opened with astonishment to see Tommy surrounded by nearly a hundred hens taking their afternoon meal. No less surprised were the birds to see anyone other than Tommy their master.

Describing this incident in his own words, Tommy said, 'T'minnet t'hens saw him wi' his bag they thow't he'd cum't for them, no doot, for ivvery yan o' them flew slap through t'window, and there I was, t'hens a gane like wildfire, nobbut God knew whar and my window gone for ivver excepting a few lile odd panes in t'corners. I ordered fellah off aboot hus business rader roughly, but he'd hard t'crash, and he was gan to t'gate when I tell't him what I thowt aboot him.'

On his return from Bowness another day he discovered 'a young sterk standing in t'corner wi' a gate round its neck. It had pushed it head through t'gate and could not git it back again and had marched itself off wi' my gate. So I gat me gate back and it gat it head back.'

Although no photograph is known to exist of this Lakeland character, Joseph Hardman of Kendal, the famous Abraham brothers, or A. Pettitt of Keswick and Gilsland would almost certainly have photographed him at some time.

My late brother John Charles Houghton was content to sketch and paint high hills.

In a career spanning half a century Joseph Hardman exposed over 60,000 photographs. These professionals climbed miles of rough country with heavy plate cameras and equipment on foot or fell pony, in search of ordinary dalesfolk, characters like Tommy, or simply superb views. Unfortunately almost all the wonderful historical array of evidence has been destroyed, but the photographs that have survived shed an authentic light on the late nineteenth-century rural world.

Tommy, in his travels, would hear the cry from the peat cutter's cart, 'ten penny as long as we've any', and the post horse of Rigg's Royal Mail Coach echoing over the countryside. In their smart scarlet coats and top hats the coachmen were a far cry from beggars, self-employed roadmen, stonebreakers, pedlars, farm workers, shepherds and travelling tailors whom Tommy would undoubtedly pass on his way.

The traditional name for a pedlar or travelling packman was Scotchman although he may not necessarily have hailed from that country. Journeying even further afield than the eggman, they too had regular calling places and were just as welcome with their ribbons, laces, pins, needles, bobbins, the far-famed Kendal Green cloth or Kendal's equally well-known brown snuff.

They slept under hedgerows, with their precious pack for a pillow, as did vagrants like Tam, of whom a photograph does exist, his sack of worldly possessions roped to his person. He carried a stout stick, wore a tam o' shanter and a long, snuff-coloured coat. Everyone also knew Tommy Dobson from Staveley, Westmorland: bobbin-turner and huntsman for fifty-three years. In order to feed the hounds he was known on occasions to go hungry himself.

Yet another Thomas, Thomas Geldart, roadman, worked all his life on making a track over Haverthwaite Moss in the days of the pack-trains. Even the village children had jobs to do, like the besom boys collecting materials for the swill-basket makers, who earned less than £1 for seventy hours' work.

Tommy sold eggs to Mr and Mrs John Richardson who lived on Highgate, the main street of Kendal, and who were married in 1806. John Richardson, born 1774, twenty years after the first stage-wagons from London replaced packhorses and eleven years before the first mail coach from London arrived, was an architect who designed a number of the town's buildings.

Not surprisingly, Tommy was greatly troubled with rats and a neglected bite from one of these rodents hastened his end. The vicar of the parish could not gain entrance but was so worried about his strange parishioner he climbed a ladder to the bedroom window.

Tired, Egg Tommy wanted to be left alone with his hen friends but not daunted, the zealot held forth at length and in grand Victorian fashion from the top of his Jacob's ladder on the virtues and consolations of religion. He had an unappreciative audience of over a hundred in what was surely one of the strangest addresses ever to be preached among the hills and one which might truly be called the sermon on the mount.

Born a century before Tommy was John Gough, known as the blind philosopher of Kendal, a great Westmorland scholar who had lost his sight through an attack of smallpox at the age of three. His countenance 'alive with thought', this eldest child of shearman-dyer Nathan, attended the Friends' School and became an expert botanist, having mastered Latin and Greek. Both Wordsworth and Coleridge knew him, the former giving him mention in his poem *The Excursion*. Gough married Mary Harrison from Crosthwaite and one of his five children became the surgeon Thomas Gough. This wonderful blind character was tutor to Dr William Whewell, the famous philosopher born in Lancaster and educated at Heversham School. To add further to his fame, John Gough's last pupil was John Dalton, the eminent scientist of the atomic theory.

I love the story of Dunny, John Peel's horse who, when the hunt was not on, used to follow his master around. Dunny was a Lakeland fell pony, fourteen hands high, who had formerly been used by a hawker, Peter Flynch, to pull his pot cart from door to door! A four-footed Cumbrian character!

ANNIE – SHEPHERDESS OF THE FELLS

Our first meeting with Annie Nelson of Gatesgarth Cottage, Cumberland, was fifty years ago when, as teenagers, my sister Sheila and I took our first holiday unaccompanied by adults. Following a week when we fell under the spell of the Lake District, a week of first sighting of flowers, birds and small mammals hitherto seen only in photographs, we two town-bred country lovers, high up on Fleetwith Pike, glimpsed Buttermere and Crummock Water lying far below, twin pearls set in amethyst mist. Bogtrotting and scrambling down scree, we arrived at the first habitation near the foot of Honister Pass – Gatesgarth Cottage.

Annie, shepherdess of the fells, in a pen drawing by Sheila Houghton, 1940.

'Annie's Corner', Gatesgarth Cottage, 1941.

No 'Teas' sign, but we knocked hopefully and thirstily, to be greeted by this greathearted lady of the fells. To two hungry girls it was Mecca. Annie's presence, as we drank cup after cup of tea and ate scone after scone, freshly baked and piled high with farm butter and homemade jam was pure delight. Little did we realise that we had stumbled upon one of Cumberland's best known characters, who hailed from a family which had farmed there for generations. That was the first of many visits and holidays at Gatesgarth. Indeed my sister was to spend long, student vacations helping Annie with teas for, as the Second World War ended, the little cottage grew more and more busy.

How we loved it: the tiny, circular, stone staircase to our bedroom; the black oak press dated 1654; the glowing iron range with polished, steel-rimmed oven; the welcome fire that never went out; the huge black kettle suspended from a hook; feather beds like clouds, on which, after climbing Haystacks or Red Pike, we slept soundly. Never have I slept better, nodding off to the cries of owls and in the dead of night hearing the blood-curdling, thrilling howl of vixen. At cockcrow, eagerly looking forward to another day and long before hikers were stirring, we bathed in the Dubbs, a deep area dug from the beck by Annie's brother who farmed at Rannerdale.

Gradually we realised her quiet fame. As shepherdess on her father's farm behind the cottage, Annie's way with the ewes at lambing time had been legendary. Following a disastrous year (no subsidies then!) Mr Nelson was forced to sell, and losing the farm to the Richardsons broke his heart. Through the good offices of the historian G.M. Trevelyan and others working for the National Trust, Annie was found a home in Gatesgarth Cottage where she became well known for her afternoon teas. She had many eminent callers: Mr Elliott, the provost of Eton College, and his wife; Professor Pigou, the economist; the sister of Alfred Noyce, so proud of her brother's part in the 1953 Everest expedition; Mrs Heelis, better known as Beatrix Potter; Jessica Lofthouse, the writer.

Beatrix Potter had been particularly interested in a fox which Annie had found injured and nursed back to health. She had a wonderful fearless way with animals, founded in gentleness. Her outhouse was home to birds recovering from damaged wings and indeed to any passing lame duck of whatever species. To call in her pretty, white Wyandottes at night she used a 'croudie' – a large metal spoon banged on a tin. All had to be gathered in for fear of 'Foxy', but one night he penetrated the hen house and snipped off every hen's head. Next morning the dreadful sight made me think there must be a case for fox hunting. Not so Annie!

Annie's range of callers was indeed wide. One regular was a tycoon from a Yorkshire Woollen Mill. Two ladies from Twining's Tea took their annual holiday in Buttermere where they stayed at The Fish but every afternoon they walked up to Annie's for tea, keen to renew acquaintance with this lady from the wilds who ordered whole tea chests of Twining's best. There was the 'Custard man', Phoebe and Jack who did creosoting and a 'gentleman of the road' who politely asked for a 'brew', proffering his Lyle's Golden Syrup tin fitted with a wire handle. At the other end of the social scale was the royal party from the Netherlands. While Princess Juliana walked over Robinson with her daughters, Queen Wilhelmina sketched.

Snowdrops, multiplying over years, were a glorious sight at Gatesgarth with large double petals, their spotless white veined with green, pushing up through the snow. Annie regularly sent a large bunch to our mother and one of her solemn duties was to give friends boxes containing eggs and snowdrops. She was the first person I knew to use mail order service, then in its infancy, because she scarcely ever left Gatesgarth. So busy was Annie with baking, sometimes two batches of bread a day and scones in the afternoon, she rarely got out for a walk. Oh, the aroma of her freshly baked bread! Only on one occasion did she accompany us. We all set off up Scarth Gap one midsummer at 11 p.m. It never went dark with Double British Summer Time.

My sister recalls only two occasions when Annie left the cottage, one a visit to Keswick for two corsets and the other a trip to Cockermouth on the great day when Annie drew her first pension, having carefully contributed, week by week for many years. Nevertheless Annie knew everything that was going on from Kentmere to Keswick as there was a wonderful bush telegraph. For example, the lady who lived alone in the big house, Hassness, was so nervous she slept with a gun under her pillow. Immensely generous, Annie had very little money, which many of the high-ranking visitors so interested in this remarkable countrywoman did not realise, perhaps because her parlour was a vision of Edwardian splendour: fresh roses in a cut glass bowl; sparkling white damask tablecloth; bevel-edged mirror on mahogany sideboard; silverware including cups won by her father in his farming days.

'Do you think she would like a telephone? Shall I get her one?' the wife of the headmaster of Eton College asked my sister.

'What she really needs,' said Sheila, 'is a water closet.'

Although Jonah from the farm dug the deep holes, in all weathers Annie had to empty her Elsan bucket. At last the miracle happened – a formidable task for it meant blasting through solid rock and preparing a septic tank.

In winter Billy the postman was Annie's lifeline. He collected her pension, brought news and, on Simnel Sunday, a lovely cake baked by his wife. Alan, Annie's brother, was a 'beck man'. These indispensable workmen prevented boulders from blocking the free flow of water from the fells.

'Car folks', in her Cumbrian dialect, wanted 'dainty presentation but not huge amounts of food'. 'Hostel boys', with their healthy appetites, were less fussy; but the most favoured customers were 'fell walkers', many of whom became her personal friends. Such people recognised her worth and what she presented and represented was more than money could buy. She was something of a guru, embodying the timeless Cumberland spirit, having known no other way of life. She was sought out by all manner of people, but her quiet courteous approach never differed, be it postman, professor, rambler or duke. I believe that Annie was sorry for people who did not live in her 'corner' as she called Gatesgarth. 'Laal Cathy' was how she referred to me and I can still see the kindly twinkle in her gypsy-dark eyes and hear the clatter of her clogs. Uncomplicated, wholesome and wholly good, we felt richer that her life had touched ours.

One New Year on our way home from Annie's we were caught in a blizzard on Honister Pass. The men at the slate quarry saw us. Not pleased that two girls were out in such weather, they told us to shelter in a hut where I suspected the dynamite was kept for we were sternly forbidden to smoke. They thought we were mad, but what I recall are the circling ravens and the wondrous shadows on newly fallen snow after the storm passed. Not for anything would we have missed those days.

Buttermere is not the same since Annie died. She would have been quietly surprised at so many affluent folks in smart cars crowding her corner, the bright paintwork clashing with her beautiful countryside. Screwing up her eyes and sucking in her cheeks (a characteristic) she once said to a workman, 'that colour shouts at you'. Her wisdom, natural goodness and country sense would benefit today's world, but the only lines we have left written by Annie are:

'Very busy. Going shepherding today for farm folks as men are away at Kendal Ram Fair. I go every year on this day.'

14

The Charcoal Burners of Furness

Charcoal burning has been carried out since medieval times in Cumbria and many other parts of England; indeed, the use of charcoal is at least as old as that of metals. Because of its intense, smokeless heat, the glass blowers of Stourbridge and the brass founders of Bewdley found charcoal indispensable. One famous diarist of old remarks on the great red glow in the night skies of Kent, which we know as the garden of England, produced by bloomeries using charcoal. Saltworkers, ironworkers, men in the hop industry, all needed it – as did the five gunpowder works at Sedgewick, Haverthwaite Low Wood, Blackbeck and Gatebeck. Furness people were known to clean their teeth by chewing charcoal but, when cheaper and more efficient means of smelting were discovered, demand waned.

Furness charcoal burners, c. 1905.

Charcoal burning, using screens for wind control.

A charcoal burner's hut, Grizedale Forest.

Fewer men could make a living out of it. In 1926 Back Barrow iron works went over to coke, marking the end of a spartan way of life that had been declining since the 1850s.

Wide, wooded areas were reclaimed by nature as small, dependent industries – about fourteen of them – closed down. It seems unthinkable that the Lake District, one of the world's most famous beauty spots, should ever have been part of an Industrial Revolution, but alongside copper, slate, plumbago and ruddle collecting went the work of the charcoal burners who lived on site, using laden packhorses to supply the foundries and factories. From afar, wisps of smoke arising from thickly wooded areas were all that betrayed their presence.

Among the burners' stock-in-trade would be 'stockers', a kind of adze for removing turf, slatted wheelbarrows for carrying branches and sacks of charcoal, long-handled iron shovels, oak baskets or 'swills', rakes and barrels of water. Hurdles covered with bracken were used as wind shelters when needed. Old photographs show these necessary relics of an ancient trade which has almost passed into oblivion and the dry, flat, sandy areas near streams with plenty of coppice woodland nearby. Life, although spartan, became more enjoyable in the warmer months when their families came out to join the burners.

Coppiced wood was formed by cutting mature trees at an angle close to the ground so that when new shoots appeared they grew straight and tall, reaching for the sunlight. The woods were cut in rotation every fourteen years. Different trees

Coppicing, Cumbrian woods.

produced different grades: ash delivered a long-burning variety of charcoal, oak, a high-grade product.

The charcoal burners lived in primitive huts made by stretching bracken and sods over a framework of branches that sloped almost to the ground. The wood for burning was cut at the beginning of April when the sap was in the branches. Thicker timber in 3ft lengths, known as shanklings, was stacked around a central pole with other lengths of wood graded according to size and thickness. The dome-shaped erection was then close-covered with reeds and dried grass, plastered together with 'sammel', a sandy, damp soil which enabled the structure to remain undisturbed throughout the burning. When the motty peg or central pole was removed a pan of glowing charcoal was brought from the hearth of the huts and placed inside the stack. Ignition worked downwards. The top was then sealed as airflow had to be controlled to produce steady smouldering. Should too much air enter, the whole stack could ignite. This was where the wind shields came in handy, protecting against sudden gusts.

After more fuel had been added from swills, the hole in the centre of the dome was sealed and a three-day vigil began. The charcoal pitstead needed constant attention. While the charcoal burners kept watch, patching with dried grass and soil any cracks in the pyramid that might appear as settling and shrinkage occurred, their families made besoms or swills. The most difficult part of all was 'dowsing' the stack – the pouring in of just enough water to cause trapped steam to extinguish smouldering branches.

In Cumbria at least three stacks at a time were tended, some, as recalled by Mr Tyson Allonby, born 1890, being nearly 10 yards across. At least twelve bracken-covered hurdles were needed for these as wind protection. The men of the Norris and Allonby families of Spark Bridge have re-enacted charcoal burns in recent years as the nation's interest in old crafts revives, but, apart from this, a once-flourishing and fascinating industry has vanished like a wraith. The old photograph from 1906 shows the 8ft dome with charcoal burners having a break. A treat was when the wives brought 'fiddle pastry'. Once ignited, heavy, white smoke soon turned to blue haze, which also died away, leaving little visible sign of the fire within. When burning had finished, after four hours the pit was raked out with a rauble and the ashes riddled. About twenty-five bags of charcoal would be recovered. The ¾in riddles would be held with sticks when hot. Holme Well Woods was the area.

FLOURISHING INDUSTRY AND OLD SKILLS

From humble beginnings, Lakeland Pennine Laundry (motto 'keen and clean') steadily expanded throughout the twentieth century to become the leading independent group of laundries and cleaners in the north of England. Set up by Miss Agnes Gibson of Kendal, who became the wife of Walter Milligan, business arrived, meeting the needs of a growing community. The centenary of laundry and dry cleaning collection and delivery vehicles was marked in 1990.

Laundry work: 'We return everything but the dirt'.

Kendal Socks, a rather clever clock. From early times there was a stocking industry in the town.

The Kendal Steam Laundry was set up in Wildman Street in 1890. From horse-drawn carts to the petrol engine. What an array of vehicles down the years!

Eighteen great landmarks in laundry work figured during that time. The Kendal Steam and Stock Ghyll Laundry merged with Grange District Laundry in 1929 when the first new laundry was built in Kendal at Stock Ghyll. Tentacles spread to Barrow, Carlisle, Lancaster, Ilkley, Skipton, Windermere, Sedbergh and other towns. As a child I can remember seeing trams in Whitehaven advertising the Whitehaven Steam Laundry – 'We Return Everything But The Dirt' and thinking that was quite funny.

The National Trust has tried to revive and encourage old crafts in Westmorland and Cumberland (now Cumbria) and in 1988 established a team of six surveyors to undertake a landscape survey. Such a detailed record of the historical importance of walls, paths and woodlands plays a vital role in planning and conserving. The list includes lost farms and the resources of fell sides: grazed by cattle and sheep, cut for peat or bracken, mined for iron or quarried for slate. They all play a part.

Splitting slate for roofs, c. 1900.

Slate workers at Threlkeld quarry, c. *1890.*

Woodlands were once felled for timber, trees used for fodder, becks dammed to power corn and fulling mills.

Since the 1700s coppicing the cropping of ash trees by cutting high enough to encourage regeneration has been common practice. It is a process that considerably prolongs the life of a tree and was useful in 'hedging and ditching' but in our time has not been so widely practised. David Thomason, foreman forester realised that slow growing lichens extended the life of the host tree and are an indicator of the degree of air pollution.

Another old skill is flag fencing, which the Trust is also keen to revive. Selected new flags have to be skilfully set into the ground and locked in by the old method taught by Justin Marsh. Behind the flags a traditional hedge is planted, the result being an excellent, long lasting field boundary. On our walks we also came across evidence of this and had the opportunity to meet dry-stone wallers.

WOODLAND CRAFTS

The West Cumbria Groundwork Trust has long been concerned to note that live hedges are rapidly disappearing in Cumbria. As a means of containing stock and sheltering wildlife, hedges have played an important part for centuries. They are functional, more attractive and more effective and cheaper than fencing. Some hedges have been found to be very old indeed. I recall finding wild cherries growing in one hedge with at least five other species, and they are great places for nest building. However they do need skilled management. It is not enough to allow hedges to grow just like Topsy.

We discovered that hedge-laying was a job for the expert, a prerequisite being a team of strong men dressed in leather and armed with billhooks and saws. Clinging ivy and brambles, along with low-growing tangled weeds, need removing first. These 'brashings' are useful later on to push into a newly laid hedge. Gradually they rot away but help initially to keep animals in and give the new hedge a start in life.

Low-growing, slender trunks require bending into an almost horizontal position, which needs to be done without breaking them. Take heart, for even ten-year-old children are successfully initiated into the art, the advantage being that some Cumbrian schools have woodland available for nature study and coppicing crafts.

The aims of the West Cumbria Groundwork Trust are to improve public awareness, to preserve and make clear the value of woodlands and the beauty of hedgerows in the Cumberland and Westmorland landscape. One thing we did notice was that the old separate names were more frequently on the lips of locals than the new boy – Cumbria.

Keeping one's own identity means a lot.

Windflowers in Brigsteer Woods, spring 1986.

15

Going Back

In the autumn and approaching winter of 2004 it rained for weeks on end. How it rained! A friend, primarily one of Eddie's but of mine too, I am proud to say, was 'watching the weather'. True to type he chose a pearl of a day. One on its own. A solitary gem amid all that welter of water. This friend, like my family and I, had plumbed grief but he put it this way: 'I have walked the road and worn the T-shirt!'

'Be ready at 8 a.m. tomorrow,' he said. Warmly dressed, armed with thermos flask and fruit, I was, and we were soon on the M6 motorway aiming for junction 37. A sparkling sprinkle of light snow on the fields added to the excitement as we passed

Kendal Holy Trinity Church, 12 November 2004. Though the earliest parts date back to the thirteenth century and an even earlier church is recorded in the Domesday Survey of 1086, most building was done when the town's cloth trade was booming between 1400 and 1600. Holy Trinity is the largest church in Cumbria and Trinity College Cambridge holds the living. (Ron Loomes)

Abbot Hall, Kendal, was built on a medieval site in the Palladian style (1759–62) for Colonel and Mrs George Wilson and designed by Carr of York. Now an award-winning art gallery, it is seen here on 12 November 2004. (Ron Loomes)

Garstang, 'The world's first Fair Trade town'. Rooks lazily flapped across a flawless, blue-as-cornflowers sky. The gateway to the Lakes, the bulk of Farleton Knott, unexpectedly, Lambrigg Wind Farm and then suddenly a phalanx of snow-clad mountains burst into view.

During the night, newly fallen snow had thickly covered the high fells. Shadows marked the gullies, and the as-yet untrodden tracks on different gradients clearly stood out. Sharply etched against a washed sky were the unmistakable shapes of the major peaks and below them the pure white Furness Fells seemingly a semi-circle sweeping to Morecambe Bay and an even deeper blue sea. 'My heart leaps up when I behold a rainbow in the sky', wrote William Wordsworth. After months and years of 'the four walls' this view was to me perfect in its loveliness and majesty – almost heart-stopping.

Beyond miles of dry-stone walls topped with snow, cows munching grass and sheep sitting there with the sun upon them seemed to breathe an air of contentment. In this part of the land it seemed all was right with the world and we pressed on, arriving in Kendal at 9.20 a.m., with a good long day ahead. Low mist over the River Kent was rising, dissipating fast. The sun thought it was summer. We parked near Holy Trinity, the parish church swathed in polythene sheeting where roof repair above the Parr Chapel was proceeding. Abbot Hall was closed, its lawns drenched in dew and autumn leaves.

Miller Bridge, Kendal, 12 November 2004. The original Miller Bridge connecting the town and Castle Corn Mill was repeatedly carried away by floods. In 1743 it was rebuilt in stone.
(Ron Loomes)

The Brewery, Kendal, 12 November 2004. This historic building is now a youth hostel.
(Ron Loomes)

The steep street leading to the River Kent and passing, on the left, the Kent Inn.

Unexpectedly, after those months of rain the Kent seemed placid, 'an amiable stripling of a river' but the mallards were enjoying it, their male iridescent plumage more glorious than anything seen on the catwalk. Flocks of white gulls swooped and screamed overhead. Looking towards Miller Bridge the skyline was broken with what seemed to be a gaudy derrick. Surprise! There was a fair in town!

Ron, my most efficient driver, changed his chauffeur's cap for a photographer's hat and was soon deftly getting shots in Kirklands and along Stramongate between the traffic flow: and more ancient inns, the Old Brewery, Doctor Manning's Yard. Besides warming the sheep, King Sol brought out the good spirits of Kendalians. They were as friendly and helpful as I recalled them from ten years previously, but camera shy. I was having little luck with my 'disposable' camera.

Near the Town Hall, by the 'Ca' Stone two gentlemen blanched and hurried off in different directions like melting snow as I attempted to explain and show provenance. We turned in at the Tourist Information office to check on changes. Gone was the Kendal Mint Cake shop but there was a factory downtown, gone too was the celebrated Pie Shop. The staff were good on information and lots of the minty cake was there for sale (useful for Christmas stockings) but one lady refused photo-taking. Was that Dad turning in his grave and chuckling? From early days it was dinned into me that I was a photographer's daughter and one had to work hard to get good photographs. I had climbed erratic boulders left over from the Ice Age, stood behind waterfalls, leap-frogged over my sister and pelted

The Call (Ca) Stone. From this historic spot outside Kendal Town Hall, British monarchs are announced when they accede to the throne. (Ron Loomes)

Shops that disappeared in about 1910 to make way for Kendal Library, Stricklandgate: James Bownass, boot and shoe maker; Harrisons, tailors and outfitters and R.W. Wiper's sweet shop famed for Kendal Mint Cake. (Kendal Library)

Curate the Revd Elizabeth Shearcroft by the black marble font in Holy Trinity Parish Church. (Ron Loomes)

down lanes in Anglesey with bucket, spade and dog. Did I not once try to milk a Guernsey cow? – all for Dad's camera. So I served my apprenticeship, but decided on this Kendal occasion to leave it to the digital expert. Mine was a wayward gene. But steady on Dad – some of your photographs are still around and I have used them!

The shops were enticingly decked for the coming festive season, but purposefully we strode on to spend an hour in the parish church, our tour accompanied by the unceasing bang of hammers on the roof. There was the black marble fifteenth-century font in all its massive medievalism, the font of years ago that invaded my dream; here the monument to artist George Romney who died on 15 November 1802, the wide aisle built specially for the Flemish weavers who brought their skills to Kendal; the town motto 'Wool is my Bread'. For photography, the light was perfect and so it was for Holy Trinity's stained glass. The windows glowed, 'making warm gules' like the one in John Keats's poem St Agnes Eve, not merely 'gule' but ultramarine vying with lemon and gold and green. When we reached Staveley we were ready for hot leek and chicken pie at Wilf's Café in the old Mill Yard close to the River Gowan and it was a 'must' to visit Watersmeet. I squelched through the beer garden opposite the Eagle and Child and gazed in delight at the confluence of the two rivers – Kent and Gowan – meeting and flowing on as one to collect more tributaries miles further down river.

Wilf's Café, Staveley, November 2004. Part of the old woodmill powered by the River Gowan. (Ron Loomes)

The confluence of the River Mint and the River Gowan, Staveley. (Ron Loomes)

St Margaret's Tower, Staveley, was built on land given by the baron of Kendal and lord of the manor in 1338. A belfry was added in 1589 and a clock in 1744, but because the area was swampy, a new parish church of St James was built on higher ground in 1865. The windows and nave of St Margaret's suffered but in 1887 the tower was restored, heightened and fitted with a new clock to celebrate Queen Victoria's Golden Jubilee.
(Ron Loomes)

At what must be a lovely spot in summer to rest with lemonade or a pint of beer and watch the ever-flowing streams, on that November day, although the sun shone strongly, I could feel the temperature dropping. I looked up at the wooded, bulky fell behind Staveley and wondered, was someone else chuckling besides Dad? Eddie the map-reader, the stalwart who encouraged me to 'onward, ever onward?' Oh the puffing and the blowing. But we did it.

Not one traveller in a hundred, seeing the graceful smoothness of Ill Bell on the Windermere side would imagine the steep, rugged drop on the eastern side into Kent dale where the springs collect in such lonely grandeur to form the River Kent. Kentmere with its 500-year-old yew tree was once described as 'a village living in a great silence for hundreds of years'.

The River Kent flows on at Staveley, November 2004. (Ron Loomes)

Another thought struck me and I smiled. Good photographers endure and tell a story. Dad was born in the 1870s and I was just ten days short of my eighty-third birthday. I felt like the traveller in that hauntingly beautiful poem by Walter de la Mare *The Listeners*:

> Is there anybody there? said the Traveller . . .
> 'Tell them I came and no-one answered,
> That I kept my word,' he said.